2 CORINTHIANS 5:17 (NIV)

*17 Therefore, if anyone is in Christ, the new creation has come:
The old has gone, the new is here!*

"Chad and Kathy's book "Marriage Advance" is a refresher for marriages who are in the midst of a battle. Their personal story by enduring eight tours of service for America is compelling. However, their most important contribution to American and International freedom will be in their new service to strengthen marriage. By living and teaching the practical principles which embody their work at Mighty Oaks and are expressed in "Marriage Advance", Chad and Kathy will become heroes."

- Dr. Ken R. Canfield, Ph.D. – Founder, National Center for Fathering

"Chad and Kathy give an honest and thoughtful look into their marriage that will inspire and motivate any couple to never quit! That's the message our culture must hear today, never quit and pursue God as the centerpiece of everything you do!"

- Michael & Amy Smalley – The Smalley Marriage Institute

"Chad and Kathy's vulnerability and honesty make this an incredible read! They open their married lives as models of what didn't work. Then they show us how turning to God through Scripture and deciding to fight and not quit turned their marriage around. Every chapter includes Marriage Builder Questions that will help couples really know their spouse and grow closer together. If your marriage isn't all it can be and you want more, read this together!"

- Jim West – Co-Founder, The Barnabas Group

"What God did to heal Chad, to heal their marriage, and to draw Chad and Kathy into a love relationship with Him, is one of the most thrilling stories that I have seen in over 30 years as a pastor. Read this book with an open heart and ask God to speak to you... I trust He will."

- Dr. Jeffery H. Wells – Senior Pastor, WoodsEdge Church

"This book shows what happens when two people are willing to fight for love. Thanks for showing us how to fight. This book is a 'must read' for everyone."

- Pastor Ron Woods – The Assembly at Broken Arrow

"This book is a sledgehammer. Chad and Kathy tell it like it is and focus on things common to all people. This is a brutally honest, God inspired, humble, and hope filled book. It will help many to accept God's gift of forgiveness again and again and not give up, to be the people God made them to be to be, and to love their spouses and have the marriages they want and need. It was an inspiration and revelation to read and a great blessing to know you two. God bless you!"

- David Eubank – Director, Free Burma Rangers, Former 2/75 Rangers and 1st Special Forces Group (A)

"28 years ago I made the best decision of my life. I married Lisa, the one, God made for me. Despite this advantage we have seen pain and sacrifice. We are still together because we let go of ourselves and submitted to God. Chad and Kathy have succeeded in outlining a clear path that we found only through trial and error. Save your marriage; Read this book!"

- Dr. Richard Wagner – Diplomate of American Board of Surgery

"In a day where marriage is under attack, Chad and Kathy's transparent stories, as told in Marriage Advance, clearly illustrate God's design for a husband and wife. Ultimately, God knows exactly what healthy marriages need to thrive. Chad and Kathy remind us all that His ultimate goal for marriage is oneness, expressed in a relationship bound together by God's holy covenant."

- Pastor David Baird – The Life Church

"Chad and Kathy are raw, real and relevant. This is more than their story, it is a window into God's transformation and the power of a choice in the midst one of life's greatest challenges.... A bad marriage. "Raw" - an un-sanitized look at marriage. Real – 100% transparency. Relevant – how they got up after being virtually knocked down. This is such a hope filled book, I recommend it to all."

- Tom Ferrell - Senior Pastor, Atascadero Bible Church

"This is not a book of theory and philosophy. It's written by a couple who have experienced life at its most broken, gritty, and desperate depths, and have triumphed with the help of God. And they have done the world a great service by telling us what they learned! Both from broken homes, dealing with childhoods of rejection, fear and insecurity, both tried to fill the hole in their hearts with all the wrong things. This did not work. As Chad often shares with veterans who are struggling with PTSD, 'If what you're doing isn't working for you, why not try something different?' Chad & Kathy tried something different: they put God at the center of their lives and of their marriage. This book will give you a practical, Biblically-based report on how they did it, and how you can too."

- Chris & Rahnella Adsit – Branches of Valor International, Christian Authors of multiple books to include The Combat Trauma Healing Manual and When War Comes Home

"Marriage Advance is one of the most helpful tools for marriage success. It takes a raw look inside a marriage that looked beyond repair, and shows the reality of Chad and Kathy's marriage struggle. By following God's biblical pattern for marriage and love, we get to witness love win as Chad and Kathy fight for what is most important. This is a spectacular book for anyone who is married, will be, or has been married, that no matter where you are in that journey it will provide Godly insight on how to make your relationship succeed!"

- Pastor Bruce Stewart, Lead Pastor, Renewal City Church

"I want the finished copy of this book NOW to give to every married couple I know and to all those under my care as a SOF Chaplain of 6 years. This transparent story of restoration can be used in every phase of marriage. It can be used as preventative, as maintenance and as restorative. Serving as a Chaplain within the SOF community for over 6 years this is the best Spiritual Resilience Model that matches all of our Ethos, Codes and Creeds and will, if embraced, rid the compartmentalization that so often plagues our Operators and their families. A MUST HAVE RESOURCE FOR EVERYONE!!!"

- Special Operations Forces Command Chaplain
(anonymous due to active service)

"Chad and Kathy's Marriage Advance tells their story of hope in Christ in a powerful, transparent way that engages their reader's heart from the opening sentences. Not only does their story grip the reader page after page, but the book also invites us to experience the life-changing power of the gospel in our marriage the way Chad & Kathy have in theirs. Written alternately from both Chad and Kathy's perspective and insight, Marriage Advance is a valuable resource for those struggling in their marriages as it provides tools for communication and Bible study. Best of all, you truly feel you "get to know" this vibrant, godly couple, and are drawn to their God as you marvel with them at the beauty He has wrought from the ashes of their marriage."

- John Foldberg, Lt. Colonel USMC (Ret.) and
Carrie Foldberg, ACBC Certified Counselor

MARRIAGE ADVANCE

LOVE NEVER GIVES UP

Chad M. Robichaux
and Kathy R. Robichaux
with
John A. Mizerak

MARRIAGE ADVANCE
LOVE NEVER GIVES UP

MARRIAGE ADVANCE is a book written and based upon the real-life experiences of the authors. In practical-advice books, as in life, there are no guarantees and readers are cautioned to rely on their own judgment concerning their individual circumstances and to act accordingly.

Chad M. Robichaux and Kathy R. Robichaux

With contributions from:

John Mizerak, Jeffery Wells, Jeremy Stalnecker, Steve & Babette Toth

Paperback ISBN: 978-0-9863193-9-6
Hardback ISBN: 978-0-9863193-8-9

Edited by: Jamison Warner
Published by: MLB Publishing

Learn more information about the authors at: www.MarriageAdvance.org

MARRIAGE ADVANCE

LOVE NEVER GIVES UP

PRESENTED TO:

____

FROM:

____

On This____________Day of______________________, 20_____

FOREWORD

Dr. Jeffery H. Wells
Senior Pastor, WoodsEdge Church

Marriage is God's creation, God's idea, God's gift. It is given for our fulfillment and for God's glory. It comes packed with the promise of joy and love and intimacy.

Marriage can be so good, but it can also be so hard. Countless couples have experienced how difficult marriage can be. Some marriages fail. Others stay together on the outside but wilt on the inside. Relatively few marriages actually thrive and flourish, fulfilling our dreams of what marriage can be.

God wants to see marriages thrive. So do Chad and Kathy Robichaux, and that's why they wrote this book, Marriage Advance.

Chad and Kathy have a remarkable story. I well remember this young couple coming to WoodsEdge, healthy, vibrant, athletic-looking. Chad was a veteran of Special Operations in the U.S. Marine Corps, and a world champion MMA fighter. You would not want to get in a fight with him!

On the outside, Chad and Kathy had a great life, three wonderful kids, a successful business. But there was also a dark side. After eight tours in the Middle East in tough places like Afghanistan, Chad carried with him some deep wounds and hurts that torpedoed their marriage.

By God's grace Kathy did not give up and neither did Chad. They were surrounded by people who loved them and walked with them. God grabbed their hearts and transformed their lives. What God did to heal Chad, to heal their marriage, and to draw Chad and Kathy into a love relationship with Him, is one of the most thrilling stories that I have seen in over 30 years as a pastor.

God not only brought dramatic personal healing and healing to their marriage, but He called them to minister to other people, especially our wounded warriors, and to help bring healing to other marriages. The way God has used Chad and Kathy has been astounding. They have deep hearts for God, they have deep hearts for our Nation's Heroes, and they have deep hearts for all marriages to thrive and flourish and glorify God.

Read this book with an open heart and ask God to speak to you… *I trust He will.*

Dr. Jeffery H. Wells

CONTENTS

INTRODUCTION

John A. Mizerak

I was first introduced to Chad and Kathy Robichaux and the Mighty Oaks Warrior Program when they spoke at The Life Church for Memorial Day in 2014. Even though I have no military experience, I was drawn to their ministry through that story of second chances, while trusting God for the future. Chad and Kathy's story describes the transformation of a marriage that had been claimed by the enemy to be destroyed, but instead, they were led to true restoration and victory. When I heard their story for the first time, I couldn't help but feel compelled to take a harder look at my own marriage.

I had experienced personal tragedy just a few short years earlier when I lost my wife of 27 years to cancer. In the face of that type of adversity, we can easily be convinced there is no hope. In 2012, I remarried and learned, first hand, about having a second chance in marriage. When a spouse dies, it's easy to get swallowed up in a pit of regret. I knew that I could have been a better husband, and I had been given a chance to prove it! I now feel compelled to challenge couples to never to give up before they have the chance to experience the marriage God intended for them. You have to hang in there a little longer and put in a little more effort. As long as you never give up and never stop trying to find innovative solutions to build a stronger marriage, *you can overcome your challenges.*

Struggling against the odds can be difficult. It is always easier to give up and surrender than to endure the hardships that come with holding on. But success can only come to those who find the fortitude to stay in the fight. *When you give up, there is no chance of success.*

Just as when a death occurs, *giving up* can also lead to regret. The moment we give up, we have zero chance of success, simply because we stop trying. As long as we hold on and keep moving forward, God will always allow us to be successful. Chad and

Kathy's stories will demonstrate that you can succeed against great odds, as long as you NEVER stop trying. In time, God will help you change the unfavorable conditions to favorable ones.

Chad and Kathy, like all successful married couples, still have *"up"* days and *"down"* days as well. Some days they are at the very top of the world and feel invincible. Still, other days, they feel defeated and fighting seems hopeless, but now, through their relationship with Jesus Christ, nothing can stop them from reaching their goals. They are reminded to allow God to change their perception. When they start to see things negatively, it means that they have allowed satan to gain a foothold. They have to challenge each other to put their trust in God to stay on the right path.

You will observe in this book that through God, we can ALL change the way we view any situation and press on once more. There is always hope in Him, a hope that allows us to persevere even through the darkest moments of discouragement.

Often the answers we crave are not immediately obvious. We may find ourselves disheartened by setbacks. But hanging on does not mean doing the same thing and expecting different results. It means trying Biblical, new, and novel approaches until we get the results God promises us we will have. Failure and mistakes are nothing more than lessons to learn. They are there to inform us that our approach is not getting the results we want. The only thing to do is to learn from our mistakes and adjust our actions until we attain our goals.

> **We can only break through our barriers and grow our marriages by not giving up and trusting God through the process.**

Join us in the journey to a strong and healthy marriage *"advancing"* toward the ultimate success God had in mind when *YOU said, "I DO!"*

John A. Mizerak

GETTING STARTED

Couples today find that being married doesn't guarantee that they will have quality time together. Chances are that you are both busy and you have to *plan to spend time together.*

Here are some ideas:

1. We believe in the power of mentorship. Find a Godly couple that would be willing to travel this journey with you. The wisdom and insight gained from those who have more experience can help you navigate these tricky waters.
2. Read one chapter and answer the questions each week, individually, and then make a date that week to cover this material with your mentors at a location away from your home. (Mix it up: maybe a coffee shop one week and a park or restaurant the next.) Put it on your calendar and treat it as a very important meeting! Don't change it for any reason.
3. We recommend that you switch off reading lessons aloud. The wife should read the odd-numbered lessons (written by Chad) with the husband sharing his answers to those questions first. The husband should read the even-numbered lessons (written by Kathy) with the wife sharing her answers to those questions first. Even though you've already read it once on your own, you will likely gain new insights or at least remember important thoughts when hearing it a second time.
4. During the lesson, maintain body contact, and focus your full attention on your spouse.
5. Be vulnerable and persevere. Everything you can imagine will get in the way of completing this study, but do it anyway.

Bottom line: *If you don't schedule time for one another, you won't have the time.*

What You Need:

- **Commitment to one another**
- **A calendar date to meet together weekly**

TIPS TO BUILD A STRONGER MARRIAGE

1. Get involved in a church together.
2. Pray together daily.
3. Spend another 20 minutes a day in face-to-face dialogue.
4. Read the Bible together at least once a week.
5. To eliminate distractions, let your children know that you two need time alone together.
6. Commit to making important decisions together.
7. When you are running errands together, turn off the radio in the car and talk with one another.
8. When you travel together, don't take work on the plane or the road. Spend time talking instead.
9. Continue Dating:
   Set aside special, regular times to continue developing your romance. Having an evening or afternoon out together twice a month is a good beginning.

   Arrange for a quiet evening at home alone once a month.

   Hire a babysitter to watch the kids for a couple hours even though you are home. This works wonders!

   Work out a deal with another couple to have them watch your kids overnight so you can have an evening alone… then you watch their children for them.

Week 1

Chasing the Wrong "Gods"

...to fill the hole in your heart

Chad

As I stood in the center of the cage anxiously awaiting the StikeForce announcer to reveal the results of the only split decision of my fighting career, my mind was racing... I virtually heard a drum-roll in my head as I knew the fight was close. *Never leave it to the judges,* I thought.

Humberto Deleon and I had put on a show for the ten thousand screaming fans in the Houston Toyota Center... it was the big stage— at one of the most high profile MMA organizations. I had gone into the fight with a perfect undefeated professional record, having submitted all my previous opponents. Humberto was a highly touted up-and-comer professional with amazing striking skills. As an accomplished grappler, all the interviews leading up to the fight had questioned my ability to stand and strike with Humberto, and my ego got the best of me.

I tried to prove my ability to take the center of the cage and trade punches and kicks with him. We literally beat the heck out of one another for three rounds. I remember landing some great Muay Thai "Teep" kicks that hit Humberto flush in the face, but just when I was feeling confident, I found myself sitting flat on my butt! I didn't even feel myself get hit, but I did, and I had been knocked down for the first time in my career.

Humberto swarmed on me, and I recall a moment of clarity thinking, *how can this be happening to me?* Knowing I had been knocked down made me angry… I knew it was time to turn it up. I abandoned all technique and got up and started fighting with every bit of aggression I could muster. I wanted the win so badly! Getting knocked down was one thing, but staying down was never an option.

As the referee raised my hand and the announcer declared me the winner, I felt like a champion once again… There I was on top of the world, on the big stage, and I looked like a rock star. Yet, reality would come back to me only moments later.

There were thousands of fans in attendance, but not one of them was my wife. Outside the StrikeForce cage and beyond the lights, Kathy and I were separated and my family was facing a terrible divorce. I had been knocked down in life, yet I wasn't willing to get up or fight back. Looking back, that moment is a sad reflection of what was most important in my life at the time. I was willing to fight with everything inside of me to get up from Humberto's devastating right hand… to press on, and win for one more notch on my record. Yet, why was I not willing to fight with the same passion and ferocity for my wife and family?

Years before I stepped into that cage in the Toyota Center, I had found myself in a dark place, knocked down by life, Afghanistan, and a long history of hardship. However, the downward spiral of my life and marriage wasn't the direct result of the historical incidents of my life, but from the way I responded to those incidents and where I went to cope, seek comfort, or even escape my feelings.

In my own experience and in observing other broken people, one of the most common pitfalls I have witnessed is people chasing the wrong "gods" to fill the hole in their hearts. Sadly, I must admit that I tried to fill the "God-shaped hole" in my own heart with everything but Him…a square peg in a round hole! Being as stubborn as I am, I tried to make life work this way and was met with continued frustration. My Force Recon Marine, square peg in a round hole, sledge hammer mentality didn't work this time…and I continued to come up empty as false idols, gods, and short-lived satisfactions left me feeling hopeless and incomplete.

I have always sought to prove myself, achieve, and move on to the next conquest. Recently, I was doing a live radio interview, and as the host introduced me, I heard accolade upon accolade: the titles and achievements from the military, law enforcement, academics…all good things, but somehow, instead of pride, I felt an overwhelming conviction. Ironically, after his long-winded introduction of me, the host commented, *"Wow…what a resume! How's listening to that make you feel?"* It was as if he was reading my conscience or God was using this unwitting host as a vessel to bring me to a new revelation. I'm sure he didn't expect my response: *"Well, thanks so much for that warm introduction. You know, when I hear all those things about me, what I hear is a man who lived a discontented life."* What a revelation for me and for this subject matter. Again, don't get me wrong; the things the guy was complementing me on were great things, but I had to question my motives! Why has my life been consumed with accomplishing one major achievement after another and never even taking time to celebrate, before moving on to the next conquest? If I'm being totally honest, it hasn't always been about humility.

When I came home from Afghanistan in April of 2007, I was completely broken. One day I was the golden boy of an elite military Joint Special Operations Task Force, doing what I believed to be the most important mission in the War on Terror, and the next, I was benched…I was diagnosed with severe post-traumatic stress disorder (PTSD)! I was pulled out of the fight, out of my role as a warrior, and removed from my team. It was devastating!

Besides my pride being destroyed, my dreams of accomplishing the mission were crushed, and I was in bad shape. I felt that if I honestly expressed my feelings, they would put me in a strait jacket and lock me in a padded room. The fear of being mentally institutionalized was terrifying to me. I felt as if I were losing all sanity and would either crack or my body would stop functioning and I would die. Panic attacks became the new norm for me. For the prior year, I had bottled up the anxiety, stress, and fears that were building up from my work, but they had finally overtaken me, and I crashed. When the floor came out from under me, there was a giant hole inside me. At that time, I didn't know that the void in my heart was a God-shaped hole that nothing else would fill.

While working with other warriors who struggle in the same way, I can see that hole so clearly now. I observe as warriors and their spouses try everything *but God* to fill that hole. These efforts to fill that void often make things worse…*much worse.* What I have learned is that you can't pour enough liquor, dump enough pills, or throw enough women, fame, fortune, adventure, or success at it! A God-shaped hole is reserved for one thing, and that is *Jesus Christ alone!* Without Him, there will always be emptiness, a longing desire, a thirst that will never be quenched, an itch never scratched, and a hole never filled. I was no different…after getting medications prescribed to numb the anxiety; I too was well on my way to finding something to fill that void.

For my entire life, I have grappled, performed martial arts, and practiced Brazilian Jiu-Jitsu. In fact, I had already fought professionally and was undefeated, so I had a head start on getting plugged into a new chapter in life. I could be the "cool guy" again! I wanted so badly to be respected, so that I could rebuild that ego I lost on some mountain on the other side of the world.

Kathy and I opened an MMA school and ran it as a family

business. We were living the "American Dream." What we didn't know was that I was not in a position to handle the success that would come with it. I was still broken, not healed by God, and certainly walking outside of the will He had for my life.

The school's success was incredible. We opened with 180 students, and in three years we had one of the biggest Gracie Barra BJJ/ MMA schools in America, with an enrollment of approximately 900 students in two locations. I had received my BJJ Black Belt in Brazil, I had won an MMA World Championship under the Legacy FC banner, and I was undefeated as a pro and top ranked in my division. The world was in the palm of my hand, and everything was perfect! In reality, that was far from the truth.

Although on the surface, everything looked perfect, my life was far from it! I was living a lie. Instead of liquor or excessive drug use, I had isolated myself in a fake world of success. I was a mess, and I was angry! My house was not a happy place, and my wife and kids were frightened of me. Kathy and I lived separate lives in our own home. I was ashamed. I still felt as if I had failed at my mission, and didn't even want to speak of my past military service. I was terrified of my mental health condition, having additional panic attacks or sleepless nights, so I ran from those fears by keeping myself as busy as possible. I had put myself in a position of zero accountability, in a world where everyone lifts you up and tells you what you want to hear, but no one tells you what you need to hear. I had chased and caught a false god of success, and it was unfulfilling. The temporary high of a moment in the spotlight not only allowed the void to remain, but it also caused it to grow. My wife and I were worlds apart, and it didn't take long for temptation to overtake me, as I did something I never thought I would do. My wife and I were worlds apart, and it didn't take long for temptation to overtake me. I turned outside of my marriage for attention and relationships with other women, which led to separation from Kathy and my family. I was facing the reality of a devastating divorce.

The path of martial arts is a good one; I love martial arts, and I'm still involved with it today. However, good medicine can be abused, and that is what I did: I used it out of context. Like many things in my life, I used worldly endeavors in an attempt to fill a void in my life that only God could fill. Once again, I was left empty and hopeless, even at the top of my Pro MMA career.

What a joy it is now to live a life fulfilled by God, who meets all my needs, heals all my hurts, and covers all my fears and anxieties… He is the only one who can fill a God-shaped hole.

Psalm 105:4 (NIV)
4 Look to The Lord and his strength; seek his face always.

MARRIAGE BUILDER QUESTIONS

1. *What other things are filling YOUR "God-sized" hole? What things have a greater priority than God in your life?*
2. *What has been "good medicine" in your life that has been abused and used out of context?*
3. *What are your priorities?*
4. *Make commitments to your spouse to refocus your priorities. Make a commitment to each other to lovingly encourage each other to refocus your priorities.*

Notes

NOTES

Week 2

Looking to Fill the Hole in Your Heart

...in all the wrong places

Kathy

I was two years old when my parents divorced. My father was granted full custody of my brother, Adam, and me. Adam was nine months older and was my best friend. Dad was a firefighter who worked twenty-four-hour shifts, leaving us with anyone he could find to watch us. He remarried when I was seven years old and began a new family with a new wife. I never felt part of *"their family,"* and started feeling like an ugly stepchild who was always in the way. Rejection reared its ugly head! Things just got worse, and by the age of ten, I moved in with my biological mother and her husband. Adam wanted to come with me, but my dad wouldn't allow him to leave, so I went alone. That experience always left me asking the questions, *"Why was Adam good enough to keep, but not me? Wasn't I good enough to fight for?"*

Being separated from my brother and best friend left me with a deep wound that I can still feel today.

My mother was a professional businesswoman, and a manager at every bank she ever worked. By the time she got home at night, she was drained from a long day's work. She would pop open her beer, recline in her chair, and kick her "puppies up" (as she would say) while she relaxed and watched TV. Dinner was rarely ready before 8:30PM. As I ate alone at the dinner table each night, she and my stepfather ate on their TV trays in the living room. I was out of sight and alone, rejected once more. There was never any conversation or the family bonding that I craved.

Although I know my mother loved me, I didn't have the attention that I longed for. She was not compassionate or involved in my life, but she had no problem controlling me. She would threaten to take away my phone (an early 1990's land-line) if I would disobey her, and she knew I felt that was torture! In order to gain some acceptance, I did everything in my power to be a "good girl!" Thank God I feared my mother enough not to become a rebellious teenager.

During this time, as I grew older, the sense of rejection continued to grow in me. As a child, other girls turned their backs on me and I was bullied, which often hurt me. A deep insecurity about making friends was being birthed. By high school, I was too afraid to experiment with all the "cool" things other kids were doing. As a senior in high school, I was very social and the captain of the cheerleading team, yet on the inside, *I felt like an outcast.*

One of the deepest hurts in life was at the time of my wedding. I did not get the "Daddy – Daughter" dance every young bride dreams of. I'm sure it was for many reasons, but my Dad didn't want to be there, around my Mom, and I guess he felt the whole wedding was a joke because I was marrying so young. Whatever his reasons were, it caused me so much pain, feeling robbed of the security of love I so desperately needed.

> ***That led me to cry out even more for that love from my new husband, putting such a weight on him.***

I met Chad when I was seventeen years old, while I was desperate for some stability. There were a few boyfriends before him, and as

I look back, I realize I was looking for affection and attention those boys could not offer me. Chad was different. He was a young U.S. Marine, and unlike the boys I had dated in the past, he was very mature. When Chad entered my life, he made me feel important. I felt as if I were on top of the world. I felt valuable and worthy for the first time in my life. My *"Prince Charming"* had rescued me from all my fears. Now I had someone to actually SHARE my life with. No more meals alone! I instantly put Chad on a pedestal. We were married one year later. In fact, I graduated high school only three weeks before the wedding, and at eighteen years old, I was already on my way to live life *happily ever after*... NOT! As all young married couples do, *we struggled!*

What had happened to my Prince Charming?

What happened to the Chad that made me feel valuable and worthy?

I began to fear Chad, and sharing my life with him was nothing like I had dreamed of. That hole in my heart was present again, and the rejection that came with that hole once again lived within me, stealing my joy. I saw myself as ugly, unloved, and not worthy of anything good. I thought something was wrong with me.

Why had I been in this spot so many times in my life?

Did I marry the wrong guy?

Did I get married too young?

What was I missing?

Psalm 27:10 (NIV)
10 Though my father and mother forsake me, The Lord will receive me.

MARRIAGE BUILDER QUESTIONS

1. *How have YOU struggled with rejection?*

2. *Were you disappointed and let down in your past? Talk about your experiences.*

3. *What have you expected your spouse to fulfill in your life that only God can give you?*

Notes

Notes

WEEK 3

UNEQUALLY YOKED

...with friends who will lead you astray

Chad

I've always been a little rough around the edges, so even as a young boy I gravitated to the rowdy crowd, the rough and tough future warriors of the world. However, I always tried to be the straight guy in the group...even though I had friends that did drugs, I never did. I continually had bad influences around me that tempted to lead me down a path of destruction, including the guys around me in my first years of the Marines. They would spend their weekends getting staggering drunk, but I refrained. I was able to hold the high ground for many years and be the "good boy" of the group, but over time, my resolve diminished and the tables began to turn.

I have heard it said, "Show me your friends, and I'll show you your future." I think when I finally veered off course, I exceeded the worst of the influences I had been exposed to. While drinking and drugs may not have been my choice of destruction, abusing my ability to influence others and betraying those closest to me, for my own selfish gain, were far more damaging. The line that I crossed, leading me to dive head first (off the wagon) directly into sin, was stepping outside of the accountability of like-minded men *who are equally yoked and offer a true relationship of authentic brotherhood.* I really didn't appreciate the brotherhood I had until I found myself alone and in the lowest and most devastating valley of my life.

When I came back from my last rotation overseas, in April of 2007, I was a mess. I had just been diagnosed with severe PTSD. I hated being labeled with a disorder, and even more, I hated that I felt weak, vulnerable, and a failure. I was extremely afraid of being exposed for what I'd become. Besides all those feelings, I was very insecure and afraid for my future. I hid behind the toughest mask I could find...a "Pro MMA Fighter," and an "MMA and Jiu-Jitsu Instructor." No one outside of my home had a clue I was still struggling, because no one could see what was really going on inside me; I was a fraud, and my conscience and insecurities didn't let me forget it. Living life as a fraud forces you to build your walls higher and your facade BIGGER. I couldn't risk exposure, and my pride continued to balloon, so I built a smokescreen of machoism and success. My MMA school flourished, and so did my fighting career.

However, while the fake side of my life grew, there were other areas that perished: my health, my relationships, my faith, and my overall well being suffered, and now my level of accountability was nonexistent. I had systematically blockaded anyone who would try to get close to see the real me...especially anyone who would tell me the hard things that I didn't want to hear but needed to hear. This created a vacuum and allowed me to be surrounded by those who just puffed me up, supporting increasingly poor choices. They fanned the flames of my ego, and I found myself being enabled by others who embraced my self-destructive lifestyle.

Attending church on Sundays was a perfectly fine way of keeping my family in check. However, I feared building friendships with men from church, due to my fear of exposure. I would say, *"Those men have nothing in common with me; they are weak."* This allowed me to control my circle of influence. I was a master at manipulating the influences in my life, and it eventually led to my own defeat.

Once I started separating from Kathy and turned to relationships with other women, she quickly recognized my manipulation. I was pretty reckless, and in many cases, I really didn't care. As a way to expedite the inevitable, I wasn't overly concerned if I got caught. Sadly, I began to realize that the men I called "friends" were willing to cover for me, instead of confronting me for my sinful actions. They clearly had no concern about my well-being or how my wife and children would be affected by my actions.

Even through those poor choices, I started to recognize that my "friends" were not really there for me. I actually wanted someone to tell me to stop, but I found myself alone and without accountability...It was a lonely place. I came to the realization that I had deliberately put myself in this isolated place surrounded by enablers.

> ***I had been in the company of like-minded men all along... the wrong kind of men. In fact, I became one of them!***

Misery loves company, because when we are doing wrong we want others to join in. It makes us feel justified not to be alone in our sin.

After Kathy and I separated, things only got worse. Even "Christian" friends wrongly encouraged me with comments like, "God has a plan for you, and will bring another woman into your life" or "You just got married too young and grew apart." Of all my influences, I can only recall one friend telling me that I needed to go home and do the right thing. Even though I knew he was right, I still ignored his challenge. Instead, I was choosing destruction.

However, when the point came to finally choose a new and healthy direction, the reality of my isolation became clear. I finally made a decision to make some radical changes to rescue my life and family. Then, I had a sense from God that I needed some serious accountability to sustain these major changes. A quick inventory of my life brought the sad realization that even though I had a thousand or more "friends" in my circle, I had no one that I could trust to hold me accountable. What a pathetic place to be! Humbly, I asked Kathy to help me find a man who could hold me accountable.

God then brought a man named Steve Toth into my life. He would not only be my mentor, but my accountability partner, and a model for what an authentic man of God and a true brother looked like. Steve is still the model of authentic manhood that I align myself with today. I now try to be a model for other men to look to, and I have Steve and other brothers who tell me what I *need* to hear, not what I want to hear. These men are true friends whom I can trust with my deepest and darkest secrets, fears, and struggles...without judgment. I'm now bonded with a brotherhood of like-minded men, equally yoked and pursuing a righteous life of character, integrity, and honor.

God created me to leave a legacy worth following in this world, and I am grateful for the revelation that I am not called to do it alone.

1 Corinthians 15:33 (NIV)
33 Do not be misled: "Bad company corrupts good character."

MARRIAGE BUILDER QUESTIONS

1. *Do you have friends who are a bad influence? Discuss.*
2. *Would your current friends take your side if it didn't line up with God's Word?*
3. *What kind of questions could you use to test a friend and a friendship?*
4. *Are YOU challenging your friends to live a more Godly life? Why or why not?*

Notes

Notes

WEEK 4

WHO ARE YOUR "TRUE" FRIENDS?

Kathy

The bottom line is that I really haven't had many friends in my life. Initially, my insecurities kept me from easily making friends, and then after I got married, Chad wanted to control who my friends would be. I think, deep down, he was really trying to protect me, because he feared that outsiders would lead me astray. Before our split, I felt guilty for having the few friends that I did have. Chad found something that he didn't like about every friend I had. I later realized that Chad's control revolved around his own insecurity and his deep fear of losing me. At that time, I can remember thinking that if I took less time for friends, I'd have more time for my family. Today, it's still a challenge for me to have meaningful friendships, but I know that I was always meant to be in community. Since I've isolated myself my whole life, it will continue to take time, prayer, and faith to allow deeper friendships to blossom in my life.

When Chad and I separated, it was the first time I had been alone. I had never been without my kids. During that time, we had to share them. When they visited Chad, I was unable to function. All I could do was to sink deeper into my depressed and heartbroken state. I was emotionally and physically broken. In order to find some hope, I began to attend church on Wednesday nights in addition to my Sunday morning routine. Although I was in church on Sunday mornings, I was not connecting with other members. Over time, while attending the Wednesday night services, The Lord connected me with a group of fun, God-loving people. This was the first time in my life that I was really in community. I finally felt accepted by someone other than my husband.

These people would pray for my marriage, my husband, my children, and me. They lovingly involved me in their group activities on Wednesday nights. We bowled and ate at my favorite Mexican food restaurant, Lupe Tortilla. I had friends for the first time and felt connected and loved. I was experiencing all kinds of laughter and joyful moments, and having friends started to feel comfortable for me. Relationships became easier. I found that these new church friends were *true friends*, people who understood that life doesn't always go the way we plan. It's much harder to stand by someone who is having a tough time, so having a friend who is strong enough to be the shoulder to cry on or hold your hand is priceless.

We've all had friends who only want things from us, but they never seem willing to give to us when we need it.

Relationships involve compromise.

Sometimes you're going to do what your friend wants to do, even though it's not quite your thing, and sometimes he or she is going to do what you want to do, even though it's not quite his or her thing. When a relationship is one-sided, we just end up feeling resentful and angry. It's not healthy. Choose friends with whom you feel a balance of give and take.

While friendships are full of compromise, it helps if you choose friends who share in a lot of your interests. It gives you things to talk about or share. It makes deciding on stuff to do easier. You don't have to choose a friend who likes every single little thing you do, but you should have some shared interests.

Even though I found these great new relationships with true friends at church, when I was home the enemy would use this "alone" time to lie to me and bring me back into a funk. Once again, I would doubt my worthiness and my beauty. I wondered why I wasn't getting asked out on dates. Chad seemed to have no problem in this area, yet I felt unwanted. At that time, I thought that if I would have a relationship with another man, I could, once again, be admired and worthy. When Chad realized my intentions, he was NOT happy! I just thank The Lord the door was quickly slammed shut, even if it was out of fear of Chad.

One of my new friends from church had told me something that I will never forget. He said, "You are an attractive girl, so guard yourself, because there will be men who will come along and take advantage of you. Be strong and continue to seek The Lord!" These words could only come from a God-loving person. These friends knew everything that Chad had done to my family and me, yet I never once heard them belittle him. On the other hand, when I would share those same stories with my old friends, they would tell me that I deserved better. These so-called "friends" told me that Chad didn't deserve me, and that I needed to divorce him. This advice seemed SO much easier than forgiving him as my church friends challenged me to do!!!!

I recognize that I am only human and very impressionable; therefore, I will most likely become like or take advice from the friends I hang out with. For example, I'm trained as a hair stylist, but I recently made a decision not to start my hair business in a certain local salon. In looking into this salon, I noticed that its image on social media attempted to appeal to the sexy, party crowd, and I knew I couldn't be part of that culture. The rent was affordable and the salon seemed to be a perfect place to build my clientele, but even though it made business sense… I had to choose to *not* put myself in a situation that could lead me away from the values of a Godly woman, wife, and mother. Chad teaches this lesson now in our ministry:

"Sometimes you have to say no to what seems to be the good things, so you can say yes to the best things, the things of God."

Proverbs 13:20 (NIV)

20 Walk with the wise and become wise, for a companion of fools suffers harm.

MARRIAGE BUILDER QUESTIONS

1. *What attributes make a great friend?*

2. *Why do you think choosing friends wisely and cautiously is a lifetime concern?*

3. *What does Proverbs 22:24–25 say about friendships? According to these verses, how does making friends with the wrong person affect us?*

NOTES

Notes

WEEK 5

WHAT IT MEANS TO BE A MAN

Chad

Kathy and I both come from broken homes, and we both went into adulthood seeking fulfillment we missed from our youth. Kathy had a deep desire to feel loved and to be rescued and taken to a safe place. She needed an environment that offered security and an assurance that she would never be abandoned. I always wanted to provide that for her, but I didn't realize how challenging that could be. In fact, it was impossible for me to do that without first identifying what I was missing and searching for. When I found it, I discovered it was the very thing that equipped me to lead my wife and to find the true source of her needs: *our God.*

It is our duty as husbands to provide the *eternal security* our wives long for. At the same time, we need to remember that true provision comes from understanding that, as a leader, all we need to do is point our wives to God as their ultimate source of security. As simple as that sounds, it took many, many years to discover how to do this. For many years, I had no understanding of the foundational wisdom it would take to achieve this direction for my wife and children.

While I didn't share Kathy's longing for love and security, I did have a yearning to be led into *authentic manhood.* My father, also a U.S. Marine, had served during Vietnam. He likely suffered the same anxieties and stresses coming home from Vietnam as I faced when I returned from Afghanistan. A PTSD diagnosis, including government support, wasn't available for returning service members at that time. Instead, many veterans of that era turned to alcohol, women, and other paths of destruction. I'm one of thousands, in the post-Vietnam generation, to grow up with either an absent or dysfunctional father who was incapable of providing a model of manhood for their sons. As a seventeen-year-old boy, I longed for that positive example. Since I didn't see it modeled at home, I thought,

> ***"Where better to learn how to be a man than the United States Marine Corps, Ooh Rah!" Wow…how wrong could I have been?***

Don't get me wrong...I LOVE the Marines! There are few things in my life that have made me more proud than having earned the title United States Marine! Yet, while the Marines do a phenomenal job of training young men for military service, they do not teach what it means to be an authentic MAN. The Marine training focuses on a concept of masculinity that leaves the impression that the measure of manhood is based on how many beers you can guzzle, how many women you can sleep with, how many fights you can get in, and how many "f-words" you can squeeze into one sentence. Sadly, with the encouragement of this type of flawed masculinity comes the loss of many Marine careers over alcohol and domestic violence incidents. I've witnessed good men who've lost rank over bar fights, lost their families over divorce due to their having committed adultery, or picked up some filthy sexually transmitted disease from some drunken, one-night rendezvous. These behaviors are contrary to the core values of a Marine: character, discipline, integrity, and honor. In fact, my oldest son, Hunter, is a third-generation Marine. When Hunter left for Marine Corps Recruit training, I wrote him this letter to remind him of this:

> *Son, you are NOT going to the Marine Corps to learn how to be a man. You've already learned that from the model that God has laid out for you. Remember, they can teach you how to be a Marine, and will, but you likely know far more than they do about being an authentic man, a Godly man of character. And, now, son, show them how to be THAT man and let God's light shine through you, to be an example to your fellow recruits and even your drill instructors. Remember, Joseph was a slave, but God gave him favor as a slave. God used him to bring hope and inspiration to Pharaoh, the king of Egypt! Even in the basement of a prison, locked away from the world, Paul was able, with God's guidance, to light a fire under humanity to build the Kingdom of Heaven. It's amazing how He can use the least of us. Just as in those moments in history, God is still working through those who believe in Him. And He can and will use a nasty lil' Marine Corps Recruit to bring hope and inspiration to each and every soul you encounter. Never discount where God may have you at that very moment, for the very reason He put you here!*
>
> *You are special and amazing!*
>
> *I'm so proud of the man you've become and of your courage and boldness for Him!*

I love the security Hunter now finds himself feeling, compared to the place where I was at that time of my life! Hunter doesn't have to struggle to find out what it means to be a man as I did. I called my dad and told him how Hunter was doing in Boot Camp. Ironically, his words were, "They will make a man out of him." I was happy to reply, "Too late...*he already is*."

Unlike Hunter, I found out what it meant to be a man much later in life, but it was after hitting rock bottom and almost losing it all. I have a good friend, who always says,

> ***"The thing about being at rock bottom is, it turns out to be a pretty good foundation to rebuild your life on."***

That is so true. It was at that time when my mentor and friend, Steve Toth, introduced me to what I had been searching for my entire life: a blueprint for manhood. It had been in front of me since I'd become a Christian. The plan is laid out in the Scriptures. By studying the subjects of *character, discipline, brotherhood, integrity*, and *marriage*, I discovered that I had to be intentional about the legacy I would leave behind. As I took an inventory of my own life, I realized a huge contrast between what the Bible taught about being a man and how I was living. However, these new truths I was learning gave me a standard to calibrate my life to *the Biblical standard.* I came to a fork in the road and chose to go toward the model of manhood that God had intended for me. However, every day I wake up to that same fork in the road. I have to choose God's way or my way. I now realize that there really is no MY way. My path is with God or without Him. I've already experienced life without God, and I never want to go back.

I have found so much joy in living the life God intended for me, but one of the greatest joys of coming into complete alignment with God's model of authentic manhood is that I am now in a position to lead my wife to find the true source of her needs… Jesus. Our job as husbands is to provide the same eternal security Kathy and most of our wives long for…*The true provision comes from accepting that, as leaders, all we have to do is to merely point our family to the One who is our Ultimate Leader.*

1 Corinthians 13:11 (NIV)
11 When I was a child, I talked like a child, I thought like a child, I reasoned like a child. When I became a man, I put the ways of childhood behind me.

MARRIAGE BUILDER QUESTIONS

1. *What form of leadership was modeled for you when you were growing up? Talk about good and bad examples of leadership you've witnessed. How did that affect you as a follower?*

2. *Read Mark 10:7– 9.*
   What realignments need to happen in YOUR life so that you can follow God's ultimate plan for a healthy marriage?

3. *Discuss past hurts that have kept you from fully engaging God.*

Notes

WEEK 6

LOOKING TO GOD FOR FULFILLMENT
...NOT your spouse

Kathy

How blind was I to think that a man could fulfill every need that my heart desired! It's not that we shouldn't dream for a husband who can love, care, and provide for us...that is something we are all designed to desire. However, our passion and longing to be swept off our feet can lead to expectations of our husbands that far surpass the roles they can assume. Wives can easily apply a standard to their husbands that only God can fulfill. When they fail us, we lose trust, security, and hope of ever being loved and provided for the way our hearts desire. We set our husbands and ourselves up for failure when we set unattainable goals for them. This can be disastrous for a marriage. It was for ours!

Chad and I met in the summer of 1994. I had just finished my junior year of high school, and Chad was in his first year of the Marines. We first met at my friend April's house. Chad was there after driving a mutual friend, Scott, to her house. Chad and Scott were stationed together two and a half hours away at the Marines base in Twenty-nine Palms, California. After Chad met me, he started telling Scott and April that he "wanted to get to know me," but at the time, I was interested in another boy and simply thought that Chad was too short!

A month or so later, I went to April's house for an unplanned visit. I had in no way "primped" to attract a boy; I was in sweats, and my hair was up in a bun. April had another friend over, and the two girls were prepping for a date. The other girl had long, bleached-blonde hair, full of curly bounce, and so much makeup on her face that I could have carved my name on her cheek. Since they were all going out, I planned to visit with April's parents. This was common for me, because I was close to them as well. However, when I saw Chad's truck pull up to the house, it hit me...*they are going on a date with Chad and Scott! They had set Chad up on a blind date! Wait, wasn't this the guy who "wanted to get to know me"?* After turning him down in the past, suddenly this "short" guy wasn't too short after all! When Chad arrived, it wasn't long before he and I were talking while he waited for the girls to get ready for their date. Within minutes, Chad invited ME on HIS blind date! He chose ME! In sweats and hair in a bun, I didn't simply tag along as the fifth wheel...I was the center of his attention! From that night on, Chad and I were together every free minute. I had met the man who was going to rescue me and make all my hopes and dreams come true. Finally, I was "wanted" by someone. Little me, a seventeen-year-old-California-girl; I had finally found myself complete.

I had longed for my "Prince Charming," and when Chad came along, I was certain I had found him. I thought Chad would be the one who could meet all my needs, desires, and wants, and that we would live happily ever after. This was a young girl's fairytale of a love everlasting. However, placing Chad on that pedestal was not only setting myself up to be let down, but setting Chad up for failure as well.

I knew of God at that time of my life, but I didn't have a relationship with Him. I didn't seek God to fill those deep hurts and holes in my heart. I didn't reach to God to fill the void of love that I was so desperate for. So, I thought Chad would be my future security and would always be there for me. When Chad came along, it was the first time that a man truly showed me love in return. I wanted to believe that if anyone could fulfill all of those things I longed for, it was Chad. These thoughts didn't really cross my mind at that time, but I know there was a deep sense of security I subconsciously expected from him.

It wasn't long before reality set in. Marriage did not come with an instruction manual, nor did we have a model of what marriage should look like. Our model of marriage had revolved around our last year of a passionate dating experience, and it was obvious, very quickly, that real life, married life, would be much different than dates, weekend get-a-ways, and romantic rendezvous. I have to admit that, initially, being a young girl living at base housing was kind of cool. I immediately felt all grown up… I now lived in my own home in a nice neighborhood and a husband with a stable job and paycheck, so there was an immediate since of stability. But wait, each day he had to leave me, and not just daily, but sometimes for long periods…weeks, months! Being the center of his attention faded quickly, and I felt as if I were competing with the special operations job that Chad loved and was so passionate about.

He was a young Recon Marine, and it seemed that he was always away at schools or in the field. That meant no phone calls and no letters, and he would be gone training for extended periods of time. Seeing the happiness Chad experienced from this job and the camaraderie he had with his teammates made me wonder …*did I make him happy, too?*

I became increasingly demanding of his time and competed for his attention. This competitiveness for Chad's time and attention continued far beyond the Marine Corps and grew into every area of our marriage. I felt Chad was choosing work and activities over me. After feeling as if I were not first in Chad's life, my insecurities returned with a vengeance. Chad hadn't removed my insecurities; they had just gone dormant. I became very jealous of both his work and then of the other women he began to spend time with. I believe all this pressure began to suffocate our marriage. It was during the time of our separation that I truly learned how to seek The Lord to meet my needs to help with my many insecurities. At that time, I was so desperate for peace and comfort that I'd cry out for God to heal my broken heart. I can remember standing with a blank stare in the shower, with water and tears dripping from my face, feeling completely hopeless about my family and about life. While standing there, I cried out audibly to God,

"Why is this happening to me? Help me! I can't do this! I need You! I can't be strong!"

I wasn't angry with God, asking Him why He was allowing this to happen. I just didn't feel that God was responsible for any of this. On the other hand, I DID want God to give me some answers about what to do next. I just wanted Him to free me from this nightmare.

In reality, I was hoping for a miracle.

With Chad now being off of the pedestal I had placed him on, I had nowhere else to turn and desperately turned to God. It didn't take long before I would see God's hand move in the broken areas of my life, as my heart started hurting a little less. I began to sleep through the night without the visions of what Chad was doing. I was able to smile again. The reality of Chad's choices that had ended our marriage was now something I was able to start releasing into God's hands. I remember saying, *"Chad is yours; this is not my burden anymore. I trust him to You, Lord. With You, I can now move toward forgiveness."* Releasing Chad to The Lord was the first step in escaping the cold, dark prison I had been trapped in. I have now discovered what forgiveness looks like: it's a picture of the same grace that Christ has demonstrated for us. My faith grew tremendously by seeing God work through me. I finally realized that He was the only means of getting my needs fulfilled. I'm so grateful that I no longer expect Chad to meet my every need. I am able to give Chad grace because I now understand that my husband is only human. He will always fall short of meeting my needs, as I will his.

As much as we love our husbands and want to believe in them, when we put our faith in men (or other people), we will always be let down. God will never let us down. He will not leave us or forsake us, but He wants to be our source, the object of our trust, security, and our affection. I now love, trust, and believe in Chad more than ever; however, I no longer expect him to carry the weight of providing a love and security that only God can give me. I don't love, desire, or respect Chad any less, in fact, I now feel more of these things for him, but I had to release him and allow God to carry the burden of change. Chad is now free to *choose* to love me and fulfill my needs and desires according to his capacity. It's so comforting and reassuring to know that my first comfort comes from a loving God who will never let me down! In fact, God is the only one who has the ability and capacity to meet my every need and desire.

Thank you, God, for loving me.

Psalm 103:1-5 (NIV)
1 Praise The Lord, my soul; all my inmost being, praise his holy name. 2 Praise The Lord, my soul, and forget not all his benefits—3 who forgives all your sins and heals all your diseases, 4 who redeems your life from the pit and crowns you with love and compassion, 5 who satisfies your desires with good things so that your youth is renewed like the eagle's.

MARRIAGE BUILDER QUESTIONS

1. *Do you feel pressure to give your spouse something you don't feel you have to give? Discuss.*

2. *When we find our fulfillment in the world, we soon discover that it is only temporary. Eventually, we need more and find ourselves back where we started. Things get old, people fail us, accomplishments are forgotten, and the applause fades.*

   When we find fulfillment in God, it is complete and permanent. Being fulfilled in Christ frees us from craving fulfillment in the things of the world, and instead, releases us to give of ourselves without needing anything in return!

   Are you finding fulfillment in God or in the world? Can you specifically name areas, people, and things in your life that you look to for fulfillment?

3. *How will your relationship change if you can trust God more than relying on each other for comfort?*

Notes

Notes

Week 7

Who's to Blame?

Chad

In retrospect, it is clear that I lived life believing the world revolved around ME. I always had a heart for others, but my selfish view of the world had me at my own center stage for many years. In our men's ministry through Mighty Oaks Warrior Programs, we ask a very simple, yet challenging question: "When did you become a man?" The answers we receive are very diverse, but all seem to revolve around a "macho" moment during their late teens or young adulthood.

In observing so many men truly transition into manhood, what I have seen to be the most consistent revelation in their lives has been a clear point where they walked away from their selfish ways and stepped into a life of serving others. However, I didn't come to this revelation the easy way. I took the long road and experienced a downward spiral in my life as I increasingly viewed the world as my adversary. Everyone was an idiot; no one "got it." I couldn't understand the world's laziness and lack of connection to reality. As my life continued to deteriorate, I desperately needed someone to blame for the state I was in. Certainly, none of this could have been my fault. I mean, if my dad had been there for me as a boy and young man; if my mom had chosen me over my step-dad; if my brother had not been murdered when I was fourteen; if my task force in Afghanistan had done things differently; if only my wife understood me; if all these people had done things differently...then, maybe I wouldn't be in the mess I'm in!

One day, after separating from Kathy and the kids, I was alone in the closet of my apartment when I began to cry uncontrollably.

> ***That was the moment I realized that it was me! It was such a clear revelation, and it hit me like a freight train.***

The reality of the choices I had made and the wake of destruction I had left behind overwhelmed me with guilt. All at once, I realized I had no one to blame for the position I was in. Even worse, at that moment, I realized how many people that I had dragged down with me. The thought that I was such a hardship to my family brought me to the conclusion that taking my own life might be the best thing for them. This terrifying thought, unfortunately, finds a home in the hopeless hearts of twenty-three veterans per day. It is horrifying to think that I was almost one of those statistics and would have left my children with that legacy. However, I had learned that one in three children who lose a parent to suicide kill themselves as well. Knowing how much my children look up to me was just enough motivation to pull me through the darkness of those distorted rationalizations.

A short time later, my wife came to my apartment and asked me a question that would not only change my life but also have a ripple effect on the lives of many others. She asked, *"Chad, how can you go to war and fight for our country and be willing to die for your buddies and train so hard for your MMA fights and show so much discipline to cut weight for competitions,* ***but when it comes to your family, you quit?****"* Ouch!!! First, she was right. Second, I had never been called a quitter in my entire life, and it stung!

All those years of pain, hate, and anger surfaced in a moment. I hit my knees in my lonely, little apartment and prayed for God to restore my feelings, take away the cold bitterness that had consumed my heart, and give me empathy and compassion once again. *HE DID IT!* I wept like a child for hours. Through God's grace, I found the will to respond to the challenge of my wife's question. I committed to apply the same character, work ethic, discipline, and loyalty that I displayed as a Force Recon Marine and as a world-class athlete to the areas of my life that mattered most. It was a complete shift of priorities. I would now fight for my faith, my character, my integrity, and my family. I would now have the same "never quit" attitude that I had confidently displayed throughout my entire professional life where it counted most.

In tackling this challenge to fight for the most important things in my life, God revealed so many things to me. One of the most important lessons He taught me was: *I was responsible for my own circumstances!* I also came to the realization that the historical hardships of my life did not have to define my future. It wasn't my parent's fault, my deployment to Afghanistan, or some series of traumatic incidents that created my current situation...*it was the choices that I made every day that dictated the circumstances of my life, and I still have control over those!*

> ***When did I become a man? I became a man when I stopped looking at the world as it related to me and started looking at it as I related to others; I became a man when I embraced an outward and selfless life and made a choice to do things differently.***

Through my quest to align my life to become the man, husband, father, and leader that God created me to be, I've come to a deeper revelation of what it means to take full responsibility for my life. Now, when I look at the flaws of those God has entrusted me to lead, I have a much different approach. Of course, as a leader, I hold others accountable, but I also assess each situation to understand how I could have done things better. I now have more patience, grace, and understanding for the shortcomings of others. This heightened understanding has been a game changer for me. Thank you God for opening my eyes to my own faults and responsibilities, and for a second chance to lead my family, the way *You intended.*

Romans 12:1-2 (NIV)
12 Therefore, I urge you, brothers and sisters, in view of God's mercy, to offer your bodies as a living sacrifice, holy and pleasing to God—this is your true and proper worship. 2 Do not conform to the pattern of this world, but be transformed by the renewing of your mind. Then you will be able to test and approve what God's will is, His good, pleasing and perfect will.

MARRIAGE BUILDER QUESTIONS

Marriage is a life-long process designed to teach you to see the needs of another person as more important than your own. It's a difficult transition because it's not natural. To think this way requires an intentional shift that can be made only through the power of God in your life. Pastor/speaker Andy Stanley (senior pastor of North Point Community Church, Buckhead Church, Browns Bridge Church, Gwinnett Church, Watermarke Church, and Decatur City Church) once said, "Marriage is a submission competition."

1. *In what areas in your life are you determined to make adjustments for improvement?*

2. *Who or what do you blame for YOUR current circumstances?*

3. *How willing are YOU to make changes?*

4. *What kind of changes can you make? Be specific.*

Notes

Notes

Week 8

My "Change-Him Plan"

Kathy

During Chad's and my separation, our children experienced what it meant to live in a broken family. The fighting, jealousy, rage, and hours of isolating myself left my children without the assurance they needed. Coming from a broken home where my parents did not get along, I knew how damaging it was for children to hear their parents argue and say horrible things about each other behind the other's back. I did not want my kids to experience the same trauma I did. Although I was hurt and angry at Chad, I knew that I had to act differently than my parents did. Instead of speaking negatively of my husband's actions, God challenged me to pray for him.

Honestly, at that time, I wasn't really praying for our marriage to be restored. I thought Chad had made it clear by his actions, that our relationship was over, but I was convicted to pray for him *anyway*. I thought that through my prayers, Chad would somehow change and become a better man. Even if he wouldn't change for me, I wanted to see him make changes for the kids, so they could see their parents get along and maybe even be friends. However, I didn't know how or what to pray for Chad.

How do you pray for someone who has hurt you so deeply?

I began reading a book written by Stormie Omartian entitled *The Power of a Praying Wife* [1].

As I searched the contents of the book, I discovered that I could choose areas in Chad's life that he needed to change and pray for them specifically! I was excited that this book showed me all the areas of Chad's life that obviously needed serious correction:

- Chapter 6, "His Temptations," *were many!*
- Chapter 10, "His Choices," *were selfish!*
- Chapter 19, "His Past," *another obvious issue!*

I then realized, I had *conveniently* skipped the very first chapter, and eventually, I had to face it…Chapter 1: "His Wife"…*What, ME? I need to change? Chad was the one who did all the damage to our marriage. He cheated on me! He caused all this mess! Why do I need to change? I didn't do anything wrong! So I thought… Thank you, Lord, for giving me eyes to see my faults in my marriage.*

As I read "His Wife," God softened my heart, and I began to see the big picture. The specific prayer in Chapter 1, *The Power of a Praying Wife*, that completely captivated me (and still does to this day) is paraphrased below:

> *Lord, help me to be a good wife. I fully realize that I don't have what it takes to be one without Your help. Take my selfishness, impatience, and irritability and turn them into kindness, long-suffering, and the willingness to bear all things. Take my old emotional habits, mindsets, automatic reactions, rude assumptions, and self-protective stance, and make me patient, kind, good, faithful, gentle, and self-controlled.... Show me where there is sin in my heart.... Help me.... to forgive him the way You do, totally and completely...I release him to change in ways I never thought he could. I leave any changing that needs to be done in Your hands... Show me how to support and respect him as he rises to that place of leadership.*

> *Make me a new person, Lord. Give me a fresh perspective, a positive outlook, and a renewed relationship with the man You've given me. Help me to see him with new eyes, new appreciation, new love, new compassion, and new acceptance. Give my husband a new wife, and let it be me.*

Give my husband a new wife? And let it be me? Wow! The Lord began to use the words of this prayer to crack open the hardness of my own heart. While reading this chapter, I began to cry! I quickly realized that I had not been the wife God had called me to be. The bitterness in my heart had been present far before my marriage fell apart. I was overwhelmed with a new perspective and said, *"OK, God, let's do this!"* My "change-*him* plan" had now turned into a "change-*me* plan." My prayer was now *"Change my heart, God, and let me see Chad the way You see him. Let me love Chad the way You love him, and let me forgive Chad the way You forgive him."*

At that time, Chad and I were still preparing for our impending divorce, but as I faithfully trusted God to help get me through the pain, He gave me the ability to begin to forgive Chad. I would never have been able to truly forgive Chad without humbling myself first and accepting my own faults for our failing marriage. I was not being naïve, or justifying Chad's actions, but merely accepting my part, because I had not been the wife that God had called me to be.

Each day, I continue to use Stormie's book as a guide to pray for my husband, but more importantly, my daily prayer is for *"His Wife"* praying to God for His continued work in me. I want to be the wife that God called me to be.

The verse below instructs wives to respect their husbands so that they can be an example of God's love and grace. This isn't to be followed just when it's convenient. Jesus did not say for us to only respect our husbands when they are being the husbands WE want them to be. Even though this is very hard to do, we as wives are called to do this all the time! The realization that now allows me to respect my husband, even when I know he doesn't deserve it, is the knowledge that neither of us is perfect!

I now lean on The Lord for the strength and grace to lead us to be the couple He has created us to be.

1 Peter 3:1–6 (NIV)
3 Wives, in the same way submit yourselves to your own husbands so that, if any of them do not believe the word, they may be won over without words by the behavior of their wives, 2 when they see the purity and reverence of your lives. 3 Your beauty should not come from outward adornment, such as elaborate hairstyles and the wearing of gold jewelry or fine clothes. 4 Rather, it should be that of your inner self, the unfading beauty of a gentle and quiet spirit, which is of great worth in God's sight. 5 For this is the way the holy women of the past who put their hope in God used to adorn themselves. They submitted themselves to their own husbands, 6 like Sarah, who obeyed Abraham and called him her lord. You are her daughters if you do what is right and do not give way to fear.

MARRIAGE BUILDER QUESTIONS

1. *Do you spend time praying for each other? Will you make a commitment to do so?*

2. *How have you tried to change each other in the past? Will you rely on God to make the appropriate changes in your spouse in the future? Make a commitment together to pray to God for changes to be made over the course of this study. What changes do you need to make in yourself in order to be the spouse He has called you to be?*

3. *Read Matthew 7:3–5 out loud and discuss.*

Notes

Notes

WEEK 9

NOT WANTING TO WORK OR WAIT

Chad

There has always been a power struggle between Kathy and me when it came to who controlled our finances. Kathy was constantly "nagging" me to follow her little rules on how and when to spend our money. I, on the other hand, was trying to impose my will to get what I wanted and do things my way. Neither agenda worked. As much as she tried, Kathy couldn't force me to conform to her tight, structured and budgeted lifestyle, or as she called it, "being responsible!" Ultimately, it would take an act of God to change my heart and thinking. Although, sometimes, God can teach us through His Word, at other times, we have to learn from falling flat on our faces. This was one of those times!

As in so many other times in my life, I finally embraced Him, and He lifted me up and allowed me another chance at doing things His way. His way includes a *life of joy* that we were intended to have. Unfortunately, many of us miss the opportunity to actually have joy in our lives. Instead, we go 180 degrees from His direction and find ourselves in another mess as we ask, "Why do we always have to learn things the hard way?"

Now, it's very clear why God had to take me on the long and bumpy road to realization. In fact, most of us don't want to take that long road. We want short cuts…we don't really want to wait and work for things; we want it all NOW. In teaching MMA and Brazilian Jiu-Jitsu, you have to invest time to reap a reward. I had a poster up at the front of my MMA school with a picture of some stairs…the first step was a white belt; then came blue, purple, and brown belts; and at the top step was a black belt. At the top of the poster it said, "Sorry, the elevator to success is out of order. You'll have to take the stairs!" Even if you're born a billionaire, there are no shortcuts in this world! There are simply many things in life that we need to work hard for. We have to invest our time and often wait before enjoying the fruits of our labor. However, things earned, are often the things most valued in our lives.

Even in my lowest of times, I would struggle with considering myself greedy or selfish. I have always been one of the most giving people I know. I am the iconic, "give you the shirt off my back" kind of guy. However, as I look back, in all honesty, the one thing that kept me from the marriage God had intended for me was that I am selfish…and it was ultimately my selfishness that led Kathy and me in different financial directions.

I can look back to many instances where I knew I was making poor financial choices. I had a clear intuition from God as He was sending up red flags, but I wanted MY STUFF now! I had to have granite countertops, an eight-foot-deep pool, a hot tub, and built-in grill; I had to have the new Jeep; the list goes on and on. When Kathy resisted and tried to do the right thing for us, I rebelled, maintaining my dominant position of authority as the "bread-winner!" I would put my foot down and draw the line, because I worked hard and deserved what I wanted, and NOW. Sadly, short-term gain never satisfies…the new car smell goes away; the pool becomes a maintenance nightmare, and the granite countertops get covered in more and more bills. Eventually, Kathy gave up the fight over finances in order to gain some peace. I actually thought that I won! How wrong could I be? The only thing that was more frustrating than not being on the same financial page as Kathy was lacking the money not only for the new things I wanted but also for the old things we had bought on credit.

After all this selfish behavior, there was finally a defining moment when God changed my view on finances. When I made the choice to be the man that God created me to be, I had to take an inventory of my life, including my financial responsibility! In doing so, God convicted me that the way I viewed money and possessions was all wrong. In my emptiness, I had again attempted to fill that hole in my heart that only God could fill. What I now know is that there is NO purchase I can make that can fill the hole that only Christ can fill.

Once my view on finances started to change, I discovered a new, Biblical understanding of money and possessions. As I started to discover the life and purpose God had for me, my selfish desires began to decrease. Instead of wanting to live for myself, I discovered a calling to live for and serve others. Eventually, this led to a new way of thinking that changed my life.

I started to view money as a tool for investment, rather than something that I could selfishly SPEND! Kathy and I were just beginning Mighty Oaks, and I began to understand the impact we were having on lives and families. I also started to quantify the costs. God showed me that $1,500 equated to a saved life and soul, as well as a family and legacy impacted for eternity. In the past, I had only viewed money as it equated to things I could purchase, but now I was thinking of money from the perspective of a *servant's heart.*

> ***This new thought process not only deeply convicted me, but radically changed the way I viewed money.***

Instead of seeing money as a means for self-gain, I learned to see money as a tool that God wanted me to use to provide for my family as well as to finance the ministry He had called me to do. This new way of thinking immediately became a way of living!

I still feel some temptation to buy things I really don't need, but each time I make one of those irresponsible purchases, I have a deep desire to be more financially responsible for the finances that God has entrusted me with.

The crazy thing is, as I look back, I was never really happy with or fulfilled by my free-spending lifestyle! Yet, I feel complete contentment now. My family members have everything they need, and as of recently, we are nearly debt-free. Now, instead of relying on credit, we even save to pay…in advance for things we want. What a concept! This new financial attitude is not something I would have done in response to Kathy's *"nagging,"* but instead this is a choice I now make. I'm choosing to be on the same financial page as my wife. This unity has not been achieved through doing things her way or mine, but instead, we seek out and discover God's way. His way truly satisfies the desires of our hearts and keeps us in unity in the way we manage the resources He has blessed us with.

Matthew 6:21 (NIV)
21 For where your treasure is, there your heart will be also.

MARRIAGE BUILDER QUESTIONS

1. *What does it mean to "trust God with your finances"?*

2. *Do you desire to trust God with your finances?*

3. *Read Hebrews 13:5. Are you satisfied with your current financial situation, or do you always want more? Discuss.*

4. *Read Matthew 6:19. Are there areas in which you could invest your money that will have an eternal return?*

NOTES

NOTES

Week 10

Give Up the Fight

...and pray instead

Kathy

We all have areas in our marriage where we want control. Personally, I have a tight hold on the finances because I'm better at budgeting and because I learned, at a young age, how to balance my checkbook, pay bills, and save. I always knew how much money was available to spend at all times. Chad, on the other hand, spent money as fast as he could. He only knew he was over budget when the ATM denied him cash withdrawals or when he would get his returned checks due to non-sufficient funds (NSF). At eighteen years old, Chad didn't even know about NSF or overdraft fees. If there was no money in the bank, he would anxiously wait for his next paycheck, unaware of any fees that would be assessed. As a young, unmarried Marine, all an empty bank account meant was simply eating at the Marine chow hall until payday. Chad and I were complete opposites in this area.

After getting married, Chad and I leased a new car, opened a credit card account, and quickly pushed it to the max! We spent money as Chad preferred, but I monitored it closely the way I preferred.

Did I mention that we were living paycheck to paycheck at that time?

Years later, I got fed up with our excessive spending and tired of the debt that we were accumulating. I found a thirteen-week course through our local church called *Financial Peace University*[2], written by Dave Ramsey. I was ready to get back on track with spending money wisely and getting out of debt. With Chad being continually deployed to Afghanistan at this time, it was easy to make all the decisions about where the money would go. My goals of financial freedom were getting closer. The only debt that remained was our school loans and mortgage.

When Chad returned, he was not too fond of my new financial program. He felt that he was entitled to spend whatever he wanted to because he was a hard worker. My husband was a very hard worker, but his desires didn't always line up with the available funds needed to raise a family and keep up our home. Even though we worked hard, we needed every penny we made to cover our bills. With my budget in place, including my Financial Peace University "cash envelope system," both Chad and the kids began to despise Dave Ramsey. Chad would say, *"Dave Ramsey doesn't cause financial freedom, he causes divorces!"* Sadly, Dave had to move out and debt moved back in.

I was so tired of trying to control our finances that I figured, *if I can't beat 'em...join 'em!* I threw in the towel and joined in the spending frenzy. I soon realized that having limited money makes other issues get worse! I wish I had stayed in the "budget" mindset and saved for the proverbial "rainy day!" Instead, it began to pour, and we found ourselves drowning financially. At the time, Chad had over $60,000 in debt for school loans from completing his MBA. One night, I woke up having a panic attack about our financial situation. I broke down and prayed to God to help us be better stewards of the finances that He had blessed us with. I was so sorry that we had been treating His provision with such disrespect.

It wasn't long after that panic-filled prayer when The Lord called us into ministry. Chad and I prayed about it and knew that our fear of total financial loss could keep us from starting the ministry that God was calling us to. Stepping out in faith and not knowing if we would financially survive should have been terrifying. In fact, everyone else was frightened for us, but somehow we knew we would be okay. It's funny to look back, but we didn't know how we would buy groceries, pay rent, or even finance this start-up ministry, but God was supplying an overabundance of faith to do His will. Instead of fear, we took on a newly found Biblical sense of financial responsibility. Suddenly, my goal of paying down our debts was less important. Shelter, food, and transportation were our main priorities. Our credit score took a *significant* dive into the abyss. I began to pray earnestly for God to take care of all of our financial needs, including our credit score. In fact, it became a true blessing to make so little in that first year of ministry in Colorado.

We started with absolutely nothing and had to faithfully depend on God to pay our bills and to survive. It was the first time our family completely trusted God for provision and didn't depend on Chad to bring in more income. The Lord not only used us to help struggling veterans and their families find freedom in Christ, but He helped us find freedom from the financial bondage that held us captive. Our faith in Christ grew tremendously during that time, as He always met our every need.

It wasn't long before we were financially on our feet, with our heads above water. Praise God! But, just as we were getting our feet firmly planted, Chad decided he wanted a Harley Davidson Sportster motorcycle. *Really God? What in the world is Chad thinking?* We had no savings, and we were still in debt. We were finally putting The Lord first in our finances and being diligent with our money. I continued to put this situation in God's hands, thinking that He would somehow keep Chad from making this horrible mistake. My heart was broken when Chad pulled up on that motorcycle. Finding out it was financed at a 26% interest rate made me downright angry! It took every ounce of my strength to keep my mouth zipped and my eyes focused on Christ. *(Although, the fact that he looked HOT on his new ride, while sporting his tattoos, helped curb my anger just a bit!)*

God showed up big time! It wasn't but two weeks later when Chad approached me and said, "I think I made a mistake!" I began to praise The Lord for doing the work that needed to be done in Chad.

> ***I didn't have to attack my husband for his selfish and irresponsible purchase. I was able to put it into God's hands, and He took care of the rest.***

Yes, the financial burden was still there, but it wasn't long before we were able to sell the bike and get back on track. I give God all glory because I can now say Chad and I are on the same page about our budget. We are nearly debt-free and no longer live paycheck to paycheck. Our tithing comes first in our finances, and we discuss all decisions for large purchases until we agree on them together.

> **Psalm 85:8 (NIV)**
> *8 I will listen to what God The Lord says; he promises peace to his people, his faithful servants—but let them not turn to folly.*

MARRIAGE BUILDER QUESTIONS

1. *The Bible contains about 2,350 verses on money. Fifteen percent of the Bible is about money and possessions; that is more than any other single topic! Look through the Bible for the answers, especially if this is an issue in your marriage.*

2. *Individually pray for the next week about your spending/ saving habits and ask God to reveal any changes that may need to happen. Be ready to share what God shows you next week.*

3. *Review www.daveramsey.com for Financial Peace University.*

NOTES

Notes

WEEK 11

HOW MUCH TIME IS ENOUGH?

Chad

Our three-month marital separation ended abruptly when I called Kathy and told her, *"I am coming home...I don't care if I have to sleep on your back porch to earn your trust back, because I will. I'm going to fix this and I don't expect anything in return."* I decided that it was up to me to repair the damage I had caused and understood that I could put NO expectations on her. Kathy reluctantly accepted with the stipulation that I would seek Biblical marriage counseling for us both. This commitment to fight, with no expectations from Kathy, would be much more challenging than I ever could have imagined. The trials ahead would stretch this new commitment to our marriage far beyond a simple momentary change of heart. It would be much more than I could endure on my own, and the only option I had in order to persevere was to follow Kathy's example of trusting our faithful God when all seemed hopeless.

In just a few days, Kathy accepted my proposal and gave me one last chance, thank God for last chances. She allowed me to forgo living on the back porch, and I moved back in with her and the family. This time, I was charged up and motivated to do the right thing. Kathy's challenging questions to me echoed in my conscience: *"...but when it comes to your family, you quit."* She was right, but I was going to change that. I wasn't going to quit on my health, future, wife, kids, or my relationship with God. I was ALL IN!

I wasn't naïve; I was expecting this transition to be hard work, but I quickly discovered that this new quest would be the toughest battle of my life. This new situation didn't make sense to me in the beginning...Kathy had prayed for me to be a new man, a husband of integrity and the Godly leader in our home. However, when I finally started to become that man, she rejected it. What is going on here? Not only did she reject it, but also it seemed to me as if she was now giving up... or trying to sabotage this new path. Wasn't she the one who wanted to take this direction so badly...for the kids, for me, for her?

> ***Was this "fairy tale" new beginning leading us right back to where we left off before our separation? Did I make a mistake by dragging the family back together so we could live the same miserable day-to-day torment we had lived before?***

The more I went out of my way to make good choices, or to build Kathy's trust and security, the more she would reject me. I would do so many little things to deliberately demonstrate my love and commitment, but now my efforts were only met with constant reminders of what I had done to her. Through her moments of anger and rage, I thought, she only allowed me back so she could make me pay for what I did wrong. I began to believe she didn't really want it to work and *I became very conflicted.*

I have been taught to fight by some of the best trainers in the world, from my instructors and senior team members in military special operations to some of the greatest MMA and BJJ coaches like Vinicius "Draculino," Brad Anderson, Carlos Gracie Jr, and Randy Couture. I have learned to fight from the best, but no one had shown me a better example of the complete dedication of a fighter's heart than my wife, who dug in, against all odds, and fought for our marriage and family. Yet, now, I felt as if she had quit. *Did she finally give up?*

In retrospect, I know she didn't… she was passing the baton of leadership. In reality, she was tired, and when she got the first glimpse of my willingness to take the reins, she handed them off quickly and completely. In turn, instead of feeling empowered, I quickly became frustrated and felt betrayed.

After about a month of this confusing behavior, I was talking it through with my mentor, Steve, and he asked me a few questions that completely changed my perspective:

> *She doesn't trust you...Does she have a reason not to trust you?*
>
> ***Yes!***
>
> *She expects you to fail and give up on her...How many times have you failed or given up on her before?*
>
> ***Every time...until now.***
>
> *She is hurt by you...why is she hurt by you?*
>
> ***The list was TOO long!***
>
> *She is angry with you...is she entitled to be hurt, angry, or even full of rage, because of the things you've done? What if it was you and the tables were turned?*
>
> ***Yes, she is definitely entitled to all those things.***

The answers were clear; Kathy was entitled to react this way. I had devastated her and had destroyed her trust in me and her security in our world. In hindsight, even though I had a better attitude and a new perspective, I was still handling her the same way I always had and I was getting the same results. I couldn't fix Kathy anymore than she could fix me. I had to turn her over to God and make the seemingly impossible commitment to show my wife the same grace God was showing me. I had to love my wife through this transition and at the same time, allow her the right to reject my efforts. I needed to let her express her hurt and anger for the past, no matter how long it took! Kathy had fought for me when I was weak, and now that she was suffering, I had to fight for her! I had to make the decision that if I had to fight for her for the rest of my life, I would do so. I came to the realization that if this process lasted a lifetime, *I would not have repaid her for fighting for me when I was weak.*

Moving forward was not easy. Kathy would snap at me in rage, but sometimes she'd let me comfort her and say things like, *"I know I hurt you and I'm sorry"* and then she'd even let me pray with her. Other times, she'd physically push me away from her, in tears. In the worst of times, she wanted me out of the same room as her, because she was too disgusted by just seeing me. It took a lot of discipline, but during those times, I'd leave the room and stay outside the door and pray for my wife. I had made a commitment and wasn't going to quit this time, no matter how hard it was.

As time went on, I noticed she started responding differently. She began to accept my love, and my new commitment to our marriage became a reality to her. It took a full year before Kathy truly accepted my recommitment. She wasn't swayed because I did everything right, but she started to notice that when I messed up, I was reacting differently.

I had begun to take full responsibility for my actions and make immediate adjustments when I was wrong. Still, to this day, there are times when I feel overwhelmed with the need to remind Kathy of how sorry I am for hurting her. I still pray with my wife and thank her for her forgiveness…sometimes while we're together and sometimes while she sleeps.

Since that first year of fighting to pull it all back together until now, I can't say it has been easy; in fact it has seemed almost impossible at times, *but it was worth it.*

I am so grateful for a God and wife who believe in second chances!

Deuteronomy 28:1-2 (NIV)
Blessings for Obedience
28 If you fully obey The Lord your God and carefully follow all his commands I give you today, The Lord your God will set you high above all the nations on earth. 2 All these blessings will come on you and accompany you if you obey The Lord your God.

MARRIAGE BUILDER QUESTIONS

1. *Are there areas in your marriage where trust has been broken? What would your spouse need to do to earn more trust? What might you need to do to earn back your spouse's trust?*

2. *Discuss those "little things" that you do to deliberately demonstrate your love and commitment to one another. Are there any "little things" that you would like to see more often? When was the last time you expressed gratitude for the "little things" your spouse does for you?*

3. *Read Psalm 27:14 out loud and renew your commitment to have patience during this time of healing.*

Notes

Week 12

Giving Him Time to Change

... and waiting on God to make those changes

Kathy

As I sit here with Chad on our back patio to write this chapter, we have to laugh! We both know that this subject certainly is not my expertise. It's not as if I entered back into this relationship expecting Chad to be radically changed, but I sure was hoping for it. Seriously, in my defense, the man's record didn't give me much hope. There had been many times that Chad had said he was a "changed man," and yet he would repeatedly fall back into his old ways. So, giving him "time to change" did not come easy for me. I understand that we are all sinners and we all fall short of the glory of God, but Chad had chosen his sinful ways over a commitment to our family too many times in the past. I had come to the point that I didn't believe a word he said. He had lost my trust! The crazy thing was, regardless of his past behavior, Chad had the nerve to be frustrated with me and even offended because of my distrust. As I tell my children, *"Your WORD is important to me! If you lie to me, my trust in you will be broken. If it breaks, I can't allow you the freedom to hang out with your friends, because I won't trust that you can make good decisions anymore."* Although I couldn't necessarily tell Chad what he could or could not do, I DID try! He would call that "nagging." My trust in him was broken, and his word no longer had any meaning.

My faith in God was strengthened during our separation. I was now beginning to wholeheartedly rely on Christ to heal my broken heart. Because I no longer had Chad on that pedestal, I was now able to see Christ clearly as the ONE to follow. I learned that I could go directly to God for everything, even finding the strength to trust Chad again. As my faith in God grew, my heart softened toward Chad. God slowly gave me back the hope needed to allow Chad back into my life.

Even though I was gaining a renewed sense of hope for our marriage, I'd be lying if I didn't admit that I was fearful that Chad would trample what was left of my heart. That fear kept me in bondage and clouded my view of God once again. The Bible says that perfect love casts out all fear, and I constantly needed to be reminded to keep my eyes focused on Christ, so the fear from the past wouldn't be able to take root again.

Satan tormented me by telling me that Chad was not worth the sacrifice. The enemy used fear to hit me over the head on a daily basis, asking me, "Why are you taking him back? What the heck are you thinking?" Fear kept me up at night as I constantly wondered who Chad had talked to or texted earlier in the day. Initially, that fear kept me from seeing any of the positive changes that Chad was so faithfully making.

Over the next year, Chad desperately tried to demonstrate that he was a husband worthy of my love and trust. When I'd lash out at him for what he had done to our family and me, he would actually hold me and pray for me. This new reaction was so different from his old ways. Instead of belittling me by making the conflict seem as if it were my fault, he would lift me up with kind words, expressing his sorrow for the pain he had caused in the past. There were times when we would be in bed drifting off to sleep and I would feel his hand press against my heart as he prayed for me.

Even though I was still treating him poorly, he would tell me how lucky he was to have me as his wife. There were so many things he was doing to show that he was not the man he used to be. Amazingly, his actions became louder than his words. Remember, Chad's words meant nothing, so to experience his consistent and loving actions slowly mended my heart. It didn't happen overnight, but I began to trust him again.

> ***Chad's transformation to becoming a "new man" happened very quickly for him, but it took me a year to be able to accept that this change was for real.***

I can remember looking at him in shock when a conflict would arise and think, *"Wow, he handled that problem well! He didn't even blow up at me!"* Chad couldn't have made this change if not for God in his life. His past attempts to overcome temptations and selfish ways had failed many times before. My demand on him to be a better husband and father only pushed him further away.

Our daughter, Haili, was in a musical recently entitled *Guys and Dolls* [3]. Her character's name was Adelaide. Adelaide had been engaged for fourteen years to a gambler named Nathan Detroit. She wanted him to straighten up and expected him to quit gambling. She was also frustrated because their wedding date was long overdue. Adelaide and Mrs. Sarah Brown (another charter struggling with love) sang a song together called "Marry the Man Today." I think this is a perfect song to explain a woman's distorted thought process about changing her man:

At Wanamaker's and Saks and Klein's

A lesson I've been taught

You can't get alterations on a dress you haven't bought

At any vegetable market from Borneo to Nome

You mustn't squeeze a melon till you get the melon home.

You've simply got to gamble

You get no guarantee

Now doesn't that kind of apply to you and I
You and me.
Why not?
Why not what?
Marry the man today.
Trouble though he may be
Much as he likes to play
Crazy and wild and free
Marry the man today
Rather than sigh in sorrow
Marry the man today
And change his ways tomorrow.
Marry the man today.
Marry the man today
Maybe he's leaving town
Don't let him get away
Hurry and track him down
Counterattack him and
Marry the man today
Give him the girlish laughter
Give him your hand today
And save the fist for after.
Slowly introduce him to the better things
Respectable, conservative, and clean
Readers Digest
Guy Lombardo
Rogers Peet
Golf!

Galoshes

Ovaltine!

But marry the man today

Handle it meek and gently

Marry the man today and train him subsequently

Carefully expose him to domestic life

And if he ever tries to stray from you

Have a pot roast.

Have a headache

Have a baby

have two!

Six

Nine!

STOP!

But Marry the Man today

Rather than sign and sorrow

Marry the man today

And change his ways – change his ways – his ways

Tomorrow!

Wow, if it was only that easy! The truth is, it was Christ who changed my husband, not me! Patiently waiting for Christ to do the work in Chad was all I needed to do. *Everything works in God's perfect timing.*

Ecclesiastes 8:6 (NIV)
6 For there is a proper time and procedure for every matter, though a person may be weighed down by misery.

MARRIAGE BUILDER QUESTIONS

1. *I don't know about you, but I am an impatient type of person and like things done in my own way and in my own time. Are you waiting for God to answer your prayers right now? If so, what are you doing in the meantime while you wait? Discuss your prayers.*

2. *What part of Kathy's story impacted you the most? Discuss.*

3. *Is there an area of your marriage that is controlled by fear? How can you focus that area back on God?*

4. *Wait patiently and trust in God and He will work things out in your life. God is faithful; trust in Him and His perfect timing. Have YOU talked to God today and asked Him to give you the desires of your heart?*

   Pray TOGETHER!

NOTES

Notes

Week 13

Fighting Fair

...winning and losing

Chad

I think it is fair to say that I'm a pretty competitive dude. As a Pro MMA fighter, I have often said that I like winning...but I hate losing even more! This attitude certainly extends beyond the MMA cage and into my life. God has definitely given me a deep desire and drive to win. However, this "winning at-all-cost" mentality hasn't always benefited me. My competitive, "warrior spirit" gift from God, has been abused and misused more than a few times. It has caused me to fight dirty with Kathy and others my entire life. Thank God (and Kathy) that I have a professional record in marriage of 1-0, but sadly, that is not the case with many other relationships in my life. I've allowed that competitive spirit to crush some relationships through my pride, unwillingness to compromise, and fighting dirty, all for the sake of winning.

Now that I've admitted to my hyper-competitive ways and my tendency to fight dirty to win a battle, please don't think that this is all one-sided in my marriage! Don't let Kathy's beautiful, sweet, innocent exterior fool you. She knows how to fight too. The combination of my desire to win and Kathy's subtle, ninja-like tactics was a recipe for disaster. Not only did she know how to push my buttons, but she also knew when to push them for maximum impact. She knew exactly what to say to send me off the deep end when I would hurt her; Kathy can be a fireplug! Our fights in the past would be gauged by who could cut the other the deepest. Most times, victory would be determined by who could scream the loudest and say the most hurtful things. Sadly, when I look back at our fights, I can't really tell you what most of them were even about. The root cause of each dispute typically went unresolved as we both quickly turned to a common goal of winning at ALL COST. I now realize that the core issue was that we were both so selfish that we made little time for each other. Our hearts and minds were so cluttered with the busyness of life that we became less tolerable of the littlest annoyances and allowed them to erupt into major wars. I love to use the analogy of a half bottle of water, versus a full bottle. You can shake the half bottle around and even with an open lid it will barely spill a drop. On the other hand, when you have a bottle, filled to the brim with selfishness, bitterness, frustration, and anger, even the slightest movement will cause it to spill. Kathy and I were both filled to the brim. We were not in unity and couldn't take the slightest "shaking" from one another.

God used this tumultuous time to teach us life-long lessons about a *covenant marriage,* the marriage that God intended for us. This covenant-marriage model has nothing to do with winning; in fact it is the opposite. The Bible talks about the marriage relationship as being one flesh, which is the unification of oneness between a man, a woman, and God.

Grasping this perspective was a game changer for us.

Understanding that we were not two individuals striving for selfish gain, but one flesh, under God, gave us the greatest tool to defeat the enemy: *UNITY!*

I heard this story once…

> *The end of days had come for satan. God gave him these last days to reap havoc on the Earth, but soon he had to close up shop. So, satan had a garage sale to sell all of his tools used, for thousands of years, to destroy mankind. As a man walked through he noticed everything had a price tag on it. There were many of satan's greatest weapons of destruction with different values. The man noticed the most expensive price tag was $100,000,000…twice as high as any other tool! The man couldn't understand such a price, so he asked satan to explain. The tool was merely a triangle shaped piece of wood and satan explained that through the years it had been his most effective tool to destroy marriages, churches, families, and legacies. Satan explained, "This is the wedge and I can use it to divide things that God meant to be together. I've even used it to separate man from God."*

Understanding that God intended for Kathy and me to be one, bonded by Him, changed the way we handled conflict in the future. As it related to our relationship, the word *fight* no longer fit into our vocabulary. I gained a new perspective as the leader of this marriage! I now had an understanding that the fight was not between Kathy and I, *but against our common enemy.*

Satan's primary goal is to separate us from one another and ultimately separate us from God. Up to that point in our marriage, satan had been successful at keeping Kathy and me on our selfish and separate paths. However, now his plan was exposed, and I began to make some changes.

One of the main changes was the way I viewed conflict. I no longer viewed a conflict in our marriage as something *between* Kathy and I, but instead, I view it as something *against* us. Each disagreement on money, how we parent our kids, sex, and major life decisions, all those "triangle shaped pieces of wood" that the devil will use as a wedge between us. Now, once we recognize there is discontentment, we stop, we agree not to let satan come between us, we seek God, and, if necessary, we seek wise and beneficial counsel from others to face the issue *together* and in UNITY!

To initiate this UNITY, we must remain in oneness with our spouses and Christ.

I know this is a very hard concept to practice, especially in the heat of a disagreement. The first practical step is to not let things get heated up, but if they do, set your pride aside and hit the brakes. Instead, shelve it for tomorrow and pray *together* that God will bring you unity in the matter. Then seek out what God has to say about it and find common ground to come together as one.

Here are a few little tips Kathy and I practice:

- *First of all, pray together!*
- *Don't go to bed mad, but go to bed in unity.*
- *Seek wise counsel.*
- *If things have gone too far, ask for forgiveness... this isn't giving in, this is just saying, "I started to head down a path that I shouldn't have. Will you please forgive me? Let's turn this around and do it right."*
- *If it is a subject you are passionate about, and you don't trust your emotions, do not have the conversation in your home. I recommend going to a public place, like a restaurant or a coffee shop, and preferably with a third party to facilitate your disagreement. You may yell and throw things in your home, but if you act like an idiot in Starbuck's, you may have more than a crying wife to deal with. Being in public, among others, is good accountability and will keep you in check.*

Satan, on the other hand, will use other people to give you bad advice, prompting you to "fight dirty!" In fact, as I counsel others, I have heard it all. Guys, especially, attempt to give "manly" advice on how to fight with your wife and not for your wife. I've been told "happy wife, happy life," and "if Momma's upset, the whole family will pay!" While these statements may be catchy, they are very far from the truth. In fact, most of the men who have shared this advice were living joyless marriages, simply co-existing with their spouses with no friendship, romance, or true love and intimacy. Compromising for a "co-existing" lifestyle with your spouse simply creates a deep-rooted bitterness that will not go away without forgiveness and an alignment of your marriage to God's covenant plan. But the good news is, we don't have to compromise! We do not have to live bitter, and we were not called to "co-exist" and just get by. If "co-existing" is what we are striving for, then we are missing out on the joyful and fulfilling marriage God intended.

The marriage covenant that God has modeled to us through Christ's relationship with the Church is not one of mere compromise. God doesn't want us to simply cave in to keep the peace with our spouses. We are called to so much more. However, to fulfill that calling and to step into the marriage God intended, you each have to look beyond conforming to one another's agendas and instead, conform to God's agenda. No one gives in, no one just compromises, but instead you both turn away from your positions, meet together in the middle of God's plan, and move forward to victory.

Stop trying to put God into your marriage; instead, put yourselves into the marriage God intended for you to experience.

Proverbs 18:2 (NIV)
2 Fools find no pleasure in understanding but delight in airing their own opinions.

MARRIAGE BUILDER QUESTIONS

1. *Are you fighting fair? In what ways do you see Chad's experiences reflected in your approach to conflict with your spouse?*

2. *Discuss your definition of "winning." Why do you feel the need to win when arguing with your spouse?*
   a. *Ask yourself:*
      i. *Why it is so important in that moment to win?*
      ii. *How would you feel if someone else argued with your spouse the way you do? Or said another way: How would you feel if someone else treated the one you said you'll love above all other humans the way you do?*

3. *Identify areas of disunity in your marriage communications, first individually, then together.*

4. *After reading Chad's marriage-unity tips in this chapter, what are some things that you need to change to "fight fair"? Name some specific ways you can create unity.*

Notes

Notes

WEEK 14

WHO'S IN YOUR CORNER?

Kathy

As Chad confirmed in Week 13, I am married to one of the most competitive men on the face of the planet! Personally, I am not competitive, but I definitely don't mind winning! However, when it comes to my marriage, I've learned it's no game. In reflection, I think my biggest challenge is that I wanted to be heard by my husband and wanted to know what I said was important to him. At times, that desire could be misunderstood as a desire to win or be in control, but that wasn't the case at all. This typical miscommunication can leave both husband and wife feeling either in competition or shut down and not heard. Both can lead to extreme frustration and eventually resentment and bitterness. In the past, this was certainly the case for Chad and me.

When it comes to wanting my husband to really listen to me, I'm not alone. While working with other women on their marriages, I see this as a common frustration. Like most women, I need to feel important to my husband. I need to know that what I have to express is important enough for him to care to listen. In the past, Chad had the bad habit of ignoring me and closing me out, because he viewed what I had to say as "nagging." That left me feeling unvalued and resentful. Because of those emotions, I would be lying if I said I was slow to anger and fast to listen. In fact, I have always struggled with that, especially when I feel I have been shut down.

However, I have found that the key to fighting fair with Chad is not to react prematurely when conflict arises. I am learning to think before I speak, instead of reacting in anger to Chad when the heat is on. Don't get me wrong, this is much easier said than done, but God has given me a new strategy that has helped me immensely. First, God has taught me to turn to Him in times of trouble with Chad. Recently, God also provided me with a secondary strategy! He has brought me a Godly friend to challenge me in a brand new way of handling conflict.

I would like to introduce you to the most incredible woman I have ever known: my precious friend and sister in Christ, Susanne Stalnecker. She is a loving wife and mother of four wonderful, well-behaved children. Her heart is pure, and her love for The Lord shines brightly. She is the type of woman I strive to be like. She makes me want to be a better wife, mother, and follower of Christ. With my insecurities and past trust issues with women, I have prayed for many years that God would bring a friend like her into my life. God knew I needed someone who would understand me. I started praying for a friend like Susanne over fifteen years ago, and she was worth the wait! She had no clue what she was getting herself into when she came into my life, but I took full advantage of this God-ordained gift of friendship.

I have always heard my husband talk about the importance of *"brotherhood,"* and after meeting Susanne; I could better understand his views. I would hear Chad mentoring other married men, telling them that calling their wives their *best friends* is a cop-out. He would continually advise these men to have other like-minded men in their lives to be fully transparent with. I have to admit that I never really understood what he meant by this. I definitely recognized that these men had needs that their wives couldn't fulfill. Now I get it! For the first time in my life, I find myself in a *"sisterhood"* with someone to share my deepest hurts and fears during times of conflict. Even though I was doing a better job trusting God with my pain, there were still times that I felt all bottled up. I wanted to keep my emotions from spilling out into Chad's world, so I wouldn't cause an explosion and hurt our marriage. God knew I desperately needed a friend like Susanne. Even today, she is a friend who listens to me cry and prays for my marriage while never condemning me. The Bible tells us to bear one another's burdens, and Susanne and I graciously do that for one another.

I can recall that the first time I reached out to her, I was in tears. I was fearful of trusting her with the information I was about to share. I was fighting with Chad and my heart was heavy. We couldn't handle the particular argument on our own. Because we are in a ministry, I was thinking, *"There is no way we can teach others how to be the men and women, and the husbands and wives that God is calling us to be, when we can't even follow our own advice. Would she think our ministry was a sham? Would she really care at all? Would she never answer another call from me?"* I was so grateful that I reached out to her. She listened to me and actually heard my pain. Susanne didn't tell me that Chad was worthless; instead, she gave me Biblical truth on how to love my husband through this conflict. She was the tool that God used to set me back on track. If she had been my mother, she would have said, "Pack your sh#t and leave him." Sadly, that is the kind of advice I had received in the past.

> ***What kind of outside influence do you have guiding your decisions?***

To this day, Susanne still answers my calls. I consider her a gift from God and a referee or my "corner woman" in the fight for my marriage. She is always there for me for guidance during the tough times. Without her friendship, I think that "fighting fair" with Chad would be much harder.

God continues to equip me to win the ultimate victory of living the marriage that He intended for Chad and me.

Galatians 6:2 (NIV)
2 Carry each other's burdens, and in this way you will fulfill the law of Christ.

MARRIAGE BUILDER QUESTIONS

1. *Do you both take time to really listen to one another? When you talk, take time to stop what you are doing, look each other in the eye, and give each other your full attention!*

2. *Who, besides God and your spouse, is in YOUR corner? Do you have friends who are Godly influences and who will take the time for you?*

3. *Do you have negative influences that may direct you AWAY from Biblical strategies for dealing with your marriage? What can you do to turn from those relationships?*

Notes

Notes

WEEK 15

FIGHT, FIGHT, FIGHT

... until you get it right

Chad

Through our ministry, I get to tell my story fairly often at churches and at events where I am working with men and their families. I have become very comfortable at being completely transparent about my past hardships and personal pitfalls. There are many reasons for my vulnerability, but primarily it's because I understand that my life's transformation glorifies God by showing where I was and where I am today. The truth is, I am so content with where God has me that it almost seems as if I am talking about a whole different person when I discuss my past. While I do still find sorrow in Kathy and my story, I don't find shame because God has allowed me to feel so far removed from the man I used to be. However, I find less grace for myself when I think of my role as a father…it's still a struggle for me to forgive myself when I think about the impact my choices had on my children.

One of the memories that I still struggle with the most is when Kathy and I called a family meeting. The kids knew there were a lot of problems between us, but they had no clue that we were at the point of selling the home and actually separating. As the kids sat down for the big news, I remember my daughter, Haili, asking what was wrong…she definitely knew we weren't announcing a family trip to Disneyland. As Kathy and I began to break the news, Haili broke into tears and was immediately an emotional train wreck. My oldest son, Hunter, was also crying, but he didn't say much; he seemed speechless. Our youngest son, Hayden, seemed to be confused and unable to process any emotion at all. I began to explain how this was best for everyone and how it was all somehow going to be okay. How selfish and naive I was! Haili became hysterical and broke down, leading to the entire family falling apart in tears. Because we were so close as a family, it was a very natural reaction for us to come together, holding each other, as we cried, to comfort one another.

How could I be so blind to what a special thing we had as a family? In the worst possible time, we were still able to bring a joy and comfort to one another, but I was too blind to see what a special bond and love for one another we had. That was the moment that I should have stopped, hit the brakes, and not allowed this destruction to go one more minute, but sadly…*I didn't.*

We moved forward, and within days, we were loading U-Hauls, as a family, headed in two different directions. In a moment, we were a separated family, living apart, broken and unsure about the future. My earlier statement was NOT true…things were not better and it was not going to be okay. My children were devastated, and I was the one who had chosen this path of destruction for us!

Thinking of where my kids could be today if I had allowed the selfish and destructive behavior to continue is still very disturbing. What was I thinking? Was I justifying myself? Was I just looking for a quick fix to my own struggles?

> ***When I think of the risks I took with my family that led us to live separate lives all because of my selfish choices, I feel shame.***

But, I thank God that He doesn't allow me to wallow in that shame. I also thank God for rescuing my marriage and saving my children from what could have been an eternal disaster.

Today my children are amazing! I am a proud dad; as I mentioned my oldest son Hunter is in the Marine Corps and still training to be an ANGLICO Marine. In Boot Camp he was the Christian lay leader and was able to minister to his fellow recruits each night, even having the privilege of leading several young men to Christ. Haili is an amazing singer and actress who is very active in our church youth group. She has even participated in a mission trip to Germany, and is planning her second trip soon. Hayden is also active in church youth group, as well as an incredible athlete, and part of the Fellowship of Christian Athletes; he plans to be a Force Recon Marine and keep the family tradition alive. All three of our kids love God and recognize what He did for our family. I'm proud to say that we never had one issue with sex, drugs, or any other major problem; praise God!

The biggest challenge we faced was when Hunter gave beer a try as a fifteen-year-old. I received a call early one morning from a close Christian friend and his wife, where Hunter was spending the night with their son, one of his best friends. That night the two boys had decided to drink some beers. My friend's son was still pretty sick and Hunter had admitted to having a beer or two, but avoided getting really hammered, because he quickly felt the alcohol's effects. None-the-less, he knew he was going to have to answer for his bad decision. Hunter and his friend were still groggy from their late-night antics, so my friend's wife suggested we let them sleep it off and address the situation later. I didn't feel as gracious and while speaking to Hunter by phone, I instructed him to drink as much water as possible, because I was on my way over with his running shoes. After a five-mile detox sprint, Hunter's response was simple; *"That was a stupid choice."*

Amazingly, that was the one major incident with my three teens. Not too bad! On the other hand, what would have happened if

Kathy and I had divorced? Where would my kids be now? It's frightening to consider! I thank God for continuously calling me back to the path He set before me. When I finally chose my family over my selfish desires, God gave me the strength to see it through. I often counsel other men who are on the brink of divorce, and sadly, I find them justifying their actions in the same manner as I once did. These men believe the same lie that I did. They believe that they are doing their family a big favor by going through with a divorce. After this lie takes root, the common justification follows: "All the kids hear and see is fighting and they don't deserve that. They will be much happier if we are apart."

THIS IS SIMPLY NOT TRUE.

This is a rationalization that supports a selfish decision. It is a common scheme used by the enemy to destroy a family. Trust me, I've been there myself, and now I see many other men facing the same lie and this faulty thought process. Statistics and research clearly show that a family that stays together produces happier and more stable children, which translates to them being much more grounded as adults.

Children are positively influenced when their parents live in the same home while modeling what a husband and wife are supposed to represent through God's design. If parents can't model those positive gender roles, then kids look elsewhere for influence. Parents often get frustrated with the paths their kids follow, but they should always remember, they first look to us for that influence. When divorce takes place, that model is forever broken! Not only is the marriage broken, but the images and models of the greatest influencers that a child will ever have are shattered beyond repair.

Believe it or not, parents are their first choice to follow. Research shows that children raised in unbroken families are more likely to go to college, maintain a strong mental and physical health, not fall victim to suicide, resist influence to use drugs or alcohol, and are more likely to stay married themselves. In contrast, children who come from divorced homes are three times more likely to be sexually active teens [4], twice as likely to drop out of high school [5], are at high risk to become pregnant or impregnate someone as a teen [6], and far more likely to engage in criminal behaviors [7] that include drug and alcohol abuse [8].

NO! You are not doing your kids a favor by getting a divorce.

Fight...fight...fight, even if that fighting in front of the kids isn't healthy, at least the fighting shows them *you have NOT quit!* Don't get me wrong, I certainly recommend getting the fighting under control and protecting your children from it, but until you do, fight on! Your marriage and your children are worth fighting for!

The key is to change the focus of whom you are fighting against. Stop fighting the ones you love most and recognize whom your true enemy is. Satan is the one who is trying to strip away everything most important to you…to steal your sons and daughters, by separating them from the flock, your family, to become fair game for his wolves.

Thank God my kids are living testimonies of the hope and restoration of a family that only Christ can bring. The future of the Robichaux family is NOW based on the strong foundation of a covenant marriage.

No one on this planet has the ability to better model the love of Christ for their children than a mother and father.

Proverbs 22:6 (NIV)
6 Start children off on the way they should go, and even when they are old they will not turn from it.

MARRIAGE BUILDER QUESTIONS

1. *Did your parents fight a lot? How did that affect you? Discuss.*

2. *Have you been affected by divorce in your life? What are some of the ways it affected you?*

3. *Discuss why kids from "unbroken" homes are more stable as they grow.*

4. *How are you modeling the love of Christ to your spouse and your kids? How do you see your spouse modeling Christ's love to you and your kids? What can the two of you do better, both individually and as a couple?*

NOTES

Notes

Week 16

God's Model for Marriage

Kathy

What child wants to see mommy and daddy fight? Because my parents divorced when I was so young, I can't even remember them being together. But I can tell you one thing: I do remember them being apart. Oh, the constant fighting! On one particular occasion, when I was about four years old, my mother showed up at my dad's house to pick up my brother and me for the weekend. Supposedly, it was not her weekend to take us; needless to say, the surprise visit did not go over well. My stepfather got involved and things escalated quickly, until the authorities had to be called. To this day, I can still recall the way I felt that day. The fear and sadness overwhelmed me as I witnessed what was happening between my mother and father. To make matters worse, I also had to watch the physical confrontation between my father and soon-to-be stepfather…it was devastating to me. Sadly, many incidents like these are etched in my memory.

My heart breaks as I sit here writing thinking of how often my children had to witness Chad and me argue and fight. I am truly ashamed of our actions. I'm truly sorry that they had to witness all our drama much like my childhood experiences. They had NO control to protect themselves from it! To make matters worse, during those times of deep conflict, Chad and I had NO regard for our precious children's spirits and how our actions might affect them forever. If only I could go back in time and do a better job of protecting them. Unfortunately, Chad's anger and my emotions kept us from making that wise decision.

Our fights were gruesome at times, especially when I found out about Chad's betrayal. I recall once when I became so enraged that I pulled the phone from his hand to find out whom he was talking to. The next thing I knew, I was tearing his shirt off. At the same time, Chad's natural reaction was to get rid of the evidence, so he broke the phone and threw it as far as he could into a nearby field. Words can't describe the chaotic scene the kids saw that day. This was just one of many horrible fights they've had to witness.

Unfortunately, the fights escalated to a point where we would not simply separate in our home after a fight, but Chad would pack up a bag and leave, as though he were never coming home. The kids would witness this over and over and were so confused. They were thinking their daddy might never come back. I want to just cry thinking about it!

The kids tried to help Mommy and Daddy cope the best way they knew how. Hunter would often attempt to calm Chad down, while Haili and Hayden would strive to comfort me. They would beg me, "Please tell Daddy you love him," or, "Can't you BOTH say you're sorry?"

During that dark period, the kids were wiser than Chad and I were. At other times, they were scared and came to me seeking protection and the security of our love. This should never be a burden precious children have to bear. They should never have their spirits and hopes broken, causing them instability. Chad and I both had lived similar childhoods under the burden of a broken home, and now we were leaving the SAME legacy to our children. Though my home was a chaotic mess, I never once spoke poorly of Chad to our kids. If anything, I would express my sorrow for what they had just witnessed and reassure them that we loved them. There were even times when I would say, *"Your dad is just having a hard time right now."*

It drives me crazy when I see parents using their kids to hurt their spouses: using their children as a tool to leverage or harm one another. While working with other couples, it is unfortunate that we often see this tactic used. Reacting, by telling the children that "mommy is a lunatic" or "daddy is a loser," is a selfish mistake. I'm so thankful that through all our faults, we didn't stoop to this.

In the end, the only person you're hurting is the child. Ask yourself…is what I'm about to say going to benefit or hurt my children? Believe me, there were many times when I wanted to express exactly what Chad had done and what I thought of him!!! Praise God that there were times that I was able to be mature enough to say, *"Let's pray for Daddy for whatever he is going through."*

Praise The Lord for the victory in our family.

Though our kids have seen brokenness, they have also seen the *healing power of Jesus Christ* in our marriage. Now they see us fighting for the things that matter most. Yes, we still have arguments, but now, they are healthy and not destructive and the kids understand that. They now see us "fighting fair" toward a common goal of unity as we make Godly adjustments in our marriage and life. Our boys have had the luxury of watching their father grow into a Godly man and leader of our family. Our daughter has been able to find security in her daddy. All our kids have seen the power of prayer and forgiveness by watching their parents pray for one another. We are so privileged to have a second chance to make things right…*to do things God's way.*

Was this transformation easy? No way! But, wow, was it worth it! Not only do we enjoy a healthier marriage, but also the kids get to experience it with us. Our kids are seeing God's model for marriage, which is something Chad and I never had growing up.

Like our parents did, many couples throw in the towel, because *working* at a good marriage is just too hard. Somehow we convince ourselves that the kids would be better off if we get a divorce. That's a lie of the enemy. How about this instead: if we stop being so selfish and if we deliberately seek to align ourselves with the marriage God intended for us, our kids will be better off.

You said that you would take your spouse "to have and hold from this day on, for better or for worse, for richer, for poorer, in sickness and in health, to love and to cherish; until death do you part." Was that just lip service? Your children are watching you! Show them how much you love them and each other by telling them that you are sorry for the hurt you may have caused during your fighting.

> ***Now is the time to show them how to fight for what matters most…For God's truth, for your marriage and for your family!***

How will your children grow and live under the proper leadership of a marriage where divorce is not an option? Only in an environment that offers security, trust, forgiveness, and a love modeled by Jesus Himself.

> **Deuteronomy 4:9–10 (NIV)**
> *9 Only be careful, and watch yourselves closely so that you do not forget the things your eyes have seen or let them fade from your heart as long as you live. Teach them to your children and to their children after them. 10 Remember the day you stood before The Lord your God at Horeb, when he said to me, "Assemble the people before me to hear my words so that they may learn to revere me as long as they live in the land and may teach them to their children."*

MARRIAGE BUILDER QUESTIONS

1. *What's your take? Do you argue in front of the kids or is it something you try to avoid? Would you argue in front of other family members? Discuss.*

2. *When you do fight, are you working toward a common goal of unity, making Godly adjustments in your marriage and life? Discuss specific ways in which you do work for unity and areas in which you lack that unity. Discuss how you might change the way you fight in order to incorporate more Godly adjustments.*

3. *Of those who have witnessed your fights…have they ALSO witnessed you pray for one another? Try bringing prayer into the equation. Discuss what that might look like for you.*

Notes

WEEK 17

LET'S DATE AGAIN

... the right way

Chad

Growing up, I never understood the Biblical context of "dating." I had no positive role models, Biblical insight, or any relational guidance on the matter. Without it ever being discussed, the desire to date, as a teenager, came from the need to improve social status and to satisfy sexual urges.

In a fallen and broken world, we are born with a propensity to sin and live a selfish life. As toddlers, most of us learned the same first words. One of those words was… *mine.* Selfishness starts early, and as we grow, we simply perfect more clever ways to get what we want. With our selfish nature and without Biblical guidance on dating, naturally, we "date" with our own agendas in mind. That was certainly the case for me.

Asking a girl to go out on a date or to be my girlfriend came with an agenda. In all honesty, I don't ever recall my vision of dating ever having anything to do with discovering or meeting the needs of the girl. It wasn't that I had bad intentions; I just never thought that far ahead. I went into relationships ALWAYS focused on what I wanted. It took a lot of time, but Kathy and I finally figured it out.

Effective dating goes beyond self-satisfaction in the moment.

Truth be told, I ended up learning more from mentoring my own sons on the subject of *"Godly-dating"* than I did from my own experiences. When Hunter became old enough to date, the girls were already lining up for him. Hunter was always a handsome kid, extremely charismatic and very confident. He has wrestled since he was four years old. When he made the varsity wrestling team his freshman year, finding a girlfriend was not an issue…or so he thought.

The moral battle began to rage between Hunter trying to be a solid follower of Christ and his desires to have a girlfriend. I'm so grateful that he had an open relationship with me, and I was able to help him navigate this conflict. Through prayer and my mentorship, Hunter came to the conclusion that there was simply no point in dating in high school. He realized that he wasn't going to get married that young and that he would just be tempted to have a physical and unbiblical relationship. So, at fifteen years old, he made a choice that made me very proud. Hunter decided there was no point in dating and realized that he would be better off just being friends with girls, thereby preventing temptation, drama, and distractions from obscuring his future goals.

It was amazing to see him make such a mature and wise choice. It was not a rule I imposed, but a choice HE made to follow God's plan for his life. His choice didn't only benefit himself. His little brother, Hayden, had been watching and followed in his big brother's footsteps, making the same choice and for the same reasons. Praise God for allowing Hunter's courage to change the legacy of the young men in our family! Through observing their courage, I came to realize that when my boys choose to engage "real dating," for a specific Biblical purpose, it would be to court their future wives. How special it will be for the fortunate young ladies when God unites them with my sons.

Not only did Hunter and Hayden benefit from the choices they made in dating, I did as well. From observing their decisions to not date or to date with a purpose, I had to really reflect on the purpose of dating or courting as it pertained to my marriage. God had brought healing and love back into my marriage with Kathy that was beyond what I had ever had before! For what seemed like the first time in my life, I was happy and didn't want this feeling to ever fizzle out! I wanted to be intentional about the future of my marriage and didn't want to leave anything to chance.

I recognized that if I wanted to "date" my wife again, I would have to do it like Hunter…with a specific purpose in mind. I didn't simply want to "check it off" my to-do list. The old form of "dating" of one hour a week here or there, or an every-Tuesday-night-dinner-out, didn't cut it anymore. When Kathy and I would get that one-on-one time, I needed to make every effort to do it purposefully and make it special, not for my own selfish desires, but to ensure, as her loving husband, I invested in my wife's needs and the health and eternity of our marriage.

My wife and I love dinner and a movie. We are both movie nuts, and if there isn't a good movie to see, we will go just for the popcorn. I can eat an entire large bucket of popcorn before the previews are even complete! Nevertheless, while we enjoy going to a movie together, these times aren't always considered meaningful dates. I also need to be intentional about spending time face-to-face with Kathy.

She and I both love to go on hikes and have long lunches together. Sometimes, we sit on the porch like an old couple and just hang out. All these examples are great dates, and while these intentional blocks of time are necessary for a healthy marriage, they're not enough for the most important person in your life.

Besides making time for regular dates, I need to make sure Kathy understands that she is the object of my affection and that I not only care deeply for her, but I also highly value our marriage. Instead of simply being satisfied with our dating "events," I do things like follow Kathy into the bathroom to drink my cup of coffee while she does her hair. Even if I'm distracted by my work, when she is around, I make it a point to stop and acknowledge her. When I'm not traveling, we always go to bed together and we always pray together before drifting off to sleep. At that time, we also pray specifically over our marriage. If I'm traveling, I will send random texts, reminding Kathy where I am, what I'm doing and that she is loved by me. She's my first thought every morning and my last thought each night. I'm in constant 24/7 pursuit of a relationship with my wife, and I make sure she knows it!

This discipline isn't always easy to maintain when trouble comes…and trouble DOES come, but when the conflicts arise, we now choose to "fight fair!"

When trouble strikes, we deal with it fairly and remember that satan is our common enemy. We are NOT fighting against one another, but for one another, toward our common goal to have unity in Christ.

Once we pull things back together, we are intentional about investing time with one another and being deliberate about advancing our marriage. My goal is to honor my wife and the covenant marriage that God has blessed me with. This mindset has changed my definition of the word "dating," which I no longer perceive as a chore, but instead, a privilege. I don't pursue Kathy because I have to…I do it because I get to. How blessed I am that The Lord of Creation would choose me to care for such an amazing woman!

Thank you, Lord, for the gift of my wife, Kathy, and the revelation that she is worth the pursuit.

1 Corinthians 13:4–7 (NIV)
4 Love is patient, love is kind. It does not envy, it does not boast, it is not proud. 5 It does not dishonor others, it is not self-seeking, it is not easily angered, it keeps no record of wrongs. 6 Love does not delight in evil but rejoices with the truth. 7 It always protects, always trusts, always hopes, always perseveres.

MARRIAGE BUILDER QUESTIONS

1. *Are YOU intentionally dating your spouse? Discuss creative ways you could start "dating" again.*

2. *How can YOU engage your spouse more? How do YOU want to be engaged to feel more valued?*

3. *Get two Mason jars, one for each spouse. Write down as many special date ideas as you can that would be a blessing to you, and put it in the other's Mason jar. Once a month (or as often as possible), plan a date night. Take turns planning the "special date" by pulling a "date idea" from the other's jar. The spouse who is responsible for that date should plan everything... from getting a babysitter to making reservations.*

   Make a commitment to have your Mason jars completed by NEXT week and let your "special dates" begin!

NOTES

Week 18

Filling Each Other's Cup

Kathy

The summer Chad and I began to date was the best time of my life. We were young and in love! I think back and see two young kids starting off in the world, just looking to be loved and wanted by someone…and thank God we found each other. I can still feel the "heebie-jeebies" rushing through me from the infatuation that I had for Chad that summer. Chad was in the Marines, based over two hours away, yet driving that distance, daily, seemed like a breeze, even though I HATE to drive! Under other circumstances, as soon as I get behind the wheel, I start drifting off and soon find myself dozing. It's amazing how a new relationship can give you the motivation to bend over backwards for your new "Honey Bunny."

Of course, it's much harder to keep that motivation as time goes by. A long-standing relationship takes hard work and effort to maintain. Sometimes it seems easier to just give up when you no longer want to go that extra mile.

When I think back to the beginning of our marriage, when the kids were young, we were financially strapped and date nights ended up being very few and far in between. Even if we could afford a nice dinner date, we didn't have family or anyone to help take care of the kids, nor the money for a babysitter. I was always afraid to ask for help. I never wanted to burden anyone else.

Needless to say, between our financial burdens and busy lifestyle, we didn't take time to invest in our marriage, much less "date." Living life on a treadmill can easily build distance between spouses. I experienced this first hand, and it wasn't long before I felt alone in my marriage and in parenting. Chad was no longer an active duty Marine, and he was terribly busy starting his law enforcement career. He would spend his weekends as a Marine Corps Reservist, taking college classes for his degree, or participating in his fighting and martial arts. He was no longer that young Marine I fell in love with the summer of 1994, when I felt like I came first.

And for me, well, I was overloaded with changing diapers, nursing, doing never-ending laundry, bathing, feeding, and on and on. Mommies know what I am talking about!!! Honestly, the last thing I wanted to do, when my kids finally went to bed, was meet the needs of my husband. I was SOOO exhausted! Most of the time, the only break I would get was when they were sleeping. That break never lasted too long because it was only a matter of time before my daughter would cry for me to come rub her legs from the intense growing pains she had, or Hunter or Hayden would be at my bedside feeling sick and throwing up. I think I slept with one eye open for many years, because I knew that one of my babies would need me before too long.

Chad was young and trying to provide for our family the best way he could, but at the time, his mindset was that his only role was to work and provide the finances to support our family. The home and children were my responsibility. Chad thought because he worked hard to provide shelter and food for our family that he was entitled to come home and check out. He was good at playing with the kids and being their friend, but when it came to the duties of parenting, he wasn't as excited. Asking Chad to do something, like give the kids a bath, would frustrate him, as he, too, just wanted to relax and take a break.

Looking back, I realize how hard he was working and how exhausted he must have been, but I was exhausted too. Chad's reluctance to help out was a devastating blow to my dream of marriage and family. Neither of us were happy with the way our life was unfolding. I was so tired and so frustrated with my life and marriage that I would retaliate by turning my back on Chad each night in bed. Chad told me once before,

> ***"The loneliest place I've ever been is in our bed with my wife's back turned toward me." It became a nasty cycle, and I had nothing left to give him, nor did I want to.***

Ladies, if what I just described seems similar to your life, I know it's hard, and you are probably thinking that you feel the same way I did…hopeless. The good news is the story doesn't end there! Our past story is not one you have to live. I have found that God has something so much better for us.

God allows us to go through hard times to mature us, but He doesn't leave us there to harm us. I have faith that He wants much more for us, but we have to choose to step into the life He has for us…*the marriage He designed for us.* I know it may be hard now, but joy is just a few choices and steps away. I pray that this book reveals those choices and steps that you need to take to improve your marriage. I hope you are challenged to meet your spouse's needs with an eager and willing heart, *no matter how tired you are.* I feel certain that you will find restoration as you learn how to lay your concerns at the Cross. In doing so, you can move forward in peace and joy in a marriage that is full of the same excitement, while experiencing those same "heebie-jeebies" you did when you first met.

When Chad and I teach our Marriage Advance sessions, he uses an illustration with two cups half filled with water. He explains that, in the beginning of a relationship, both cups have an equal amount of water. The water represents all the things you do for each other and how you are meeting each other's needs. As Chad pours the water back and forth, one fills the other's cup and then the other returns the gesture.

For example, Chad might take me for a weekend getaway and make me feel like a princess. Well, he just poured some of his water into my cup, and I feel so loved that I, in turn, make him a steak dinner. I just filled his cup! It's a "win-win scenario"... simple, right? Not so fast...filling each other's cup is a breeze in the beginning of the relationship because we are easily satisfied and eager to please. However, as time goes by, the infatuation fades, and the real needs are often unmet.

Because we rarely understand the other's deepest needs, we often miss the mark of filling one another's cup. Soon, the bitterness of your cup not getting filled steals your desire to fill your partner's cup. One spouse either keeps giving until there is nothing left to give, or he or she stops giving and shuts his or her spouse off. This pushes your spouse to look elsewhere to have his or her cup filled and ultimately leaves you both feeling empty. Ultimately, this is yet another reminder that only Christ can really fill our cups. He's the one to whom we should look to be filled because He's the only one capable.

Remember, we mentioned in the beginning of this book: *our spouses can't meet all of our needs.* We cannot expect our spouses to fill a need that only God can fill. However, the act of filling each other's cup is an intentional act that can be done with love, while constantly pursuing one another as you did in the beginning of your relationship. As hard as it may be and undeserving as you feel your spouse is, you must make him or her a priority. You need to continue to learn about one another's needs and desires and make *the choice* to fulfill those needs. It takes a lot of grace, patience, compassion, and communication to learn each other's needs and desires. Then it takes even more time to make the investment to meet those needs for one another.

Where do you focus your time and energy?

Make "dating" and spending time together a priority. As much as I love going to dinner and a movie with Chad, my ideal date with him is a walk on the beach with his arm around me. When he spends that kind of intimate time with me, I feel as if he's making the statement, "This is my girl." I love just sitting with him on the back patio, overlooking the lake on a beautiful sunny day. This time is so special for us, because there are few distractions. All this is to say, simply being in Chad's presence on a regular basis and feeling as if I am a priority in his life is now enough to fill my cup. After twenty years of marriage, through those uninterrupted moments, we are continuing to learn more about each other and how to better love and meet each other's needs.

This new perspective in my marriage has brought me more than hope; *it has brought me joy and fulfillment! I now LOVE to meet Chad's needs!* Praise God that He renewed my heart and showed me that Chad's needs matter more than my own. Even though the kids are older and I am no longer pulled in a million different directions by their demanding schedules, Chad and I still need to be vigilant about focusing on one another.

Remember, in all stages of life, we have demands that can lead us away from focusing on our marriages. However, no matter what stage of life you find yourself in and no matter your current demands, in order to be the spouse God has called you to be, you have to choose to be deliberate about investing the time and energy into your marriage.

John 15:12–14 (NIV)
12 My command is this: Love each other as I have loved you. 13 Greater love has no one than this: to lay down one's life for one's friends. 14 You are my friends if you do what I command.

MARRIAGE BUILDER QUESTIONS

1. *Talk about how you felt when you first met. What were the things that made you feel special to the other?*

2. *What choices and steps are you willing to take to fill the other's "cup" now?*

3. *Ultimately, for a marriage to be successful, the husband and wife must include God as a partner. They must acknowledge God as Supreme in their lives and together yield to what God instructs in the Bible about marriage. Read Malachi 2:14 and discuss.*

Notes

Notes

WEEK 19

WITHOUT TRUST

...there can never be true oneness

Chad

I can remember how angry I would get when Kathy would grab my phone to check my calls, text messages, and emails to see to whom I had been talking. She would even scour the trash box and search for the deleted info. I felt under constant interrogation and surveillance by someone who was supposed to trust me and love me with all her heart. I thought, *"What right did she have to constantly accuse me and question my integrity and character?"* The truth was, a lot of the time, her fear-based accusations were wrong…but on the other hand, she was often right. However, regardless of whether she was right or wrong, critical or insecure, none of that should have mattered. Did she have the right to look at my phone, check my emails, ask me where I was and who I was with? Absolutely! She is my wife, and if she is insecure, then it is my job to build her security and trust in me and in our marriage. Nevertheless, at the time, that rationale was the furthest thing from my mind. I was defending myself, (even if I was guilty) while also allowing my anger at the accusations to bring division between us. There were times I could remember thinking, *"Well, if she is going to constantly accuse me of these things, then why not do them?"* In retrospect, many of Kathy's insecurities were warranted, and if I wasn't already doing what she was suspecting me of, I was only one step away from it. My thought process at the time was, *"With this constant conflict, jealousy and accusations, there is no way this marriage will last anyway!"* The lack of trust between Kathy and me constantly kept me in the mindset that we would never work out our differences and eventually we'd end up like everyone else…divorced. This led me to a position in our marriage where I only had one foot in and the other was already out the door. Plan B was always lurking.

I NOW know there can be NO PLAN B! You have to be ALL IN with Plan A, or you are already set up to fail.

Make a pre-determined choice today that Plan B is off the table and doesn't exist, so that you can put all your energy into the only plan that matters for your marriage: Plan A.

My background in military special operations and law enforcement included a lot of undercover work, aliases, running surveillance detection routes (SRDs), switching cell phone SIM cards, and living lies…so I thought I was pretty sly! As a trained professional and after facing foreign intelligence agents, criminals, and terrorist adversaries for a living, I could certainly take the pressure of a suspicious wife. Not really! When I was hiding my inappropriate lifestyle from Kathy, I lived in constant fear of being exposed. It was exhausting! I was constantly on the defense, and my actions fed Kathy's insecurities and lack of trust in me. As she mentioned earlier in this book, she was already a jealous person, and now she had just cause! We were in a toxic environment and our trust and my actions were spinning out of control and headed for a disastrous end.

After reading so many of our stories so far, you already know my dirty little secrets, what they led to, and what my choices almost cost me…I won't make you relive that this week. However, as I look back now, it is no wonder we weren't happy and couldn't find joy or unity. *Without trust, there simply can't be true oneness.* I never understood what people meant before when I heard them speak about "one flesh." When Kathy and I separated, I finally understood. Suddenly, this woman whom I didn't want to be with was gone, and I felt as if a part of me was missing…I felt as if I lost my legs and would need to learn to walk again. I then realized that if I were ever to have her back, I had to earn her trust.

> ***Through that earned trust, there would be a chance to finally establish "true oneness" and a marriage relationship unified by God.***

I'm sure you've heard the analogy of a rope of three cords. *(Ecclesiastes 4:12).* Each cord can be easily broken on its own, but three cords, twisted together, make that rope unbreakable by any man. It's incredible that the rope's strength is not three times stronger, but exponentially stronger. Those three cords in a marriage are the husband, the wife, and God…and what intertwines them is the trust and faith they share. That's what we were lacking and why establishing Kathy's trust was so crucial to the future success of our marriage. Kathy and I had to be unified together with God, in a NEW establishment of trust and faith.

This process was not an easy one. I had committed some serious acts of disrespect, and earning Kathy's trust back would be an uphill battle, but with God's help, I was determined. Day by day, moment-by-moment, I did what it took to show that my loyalty to both her and our marriage was the real deal. We were now in a covenant marriage, and we were linked with God for a lifetime!

Divorce was no longer an option; there was no Plan B. My efforts would not be accomplished by my words alone. As we began to rebuild our marriage, my word meant nothing to Kathy. Initially, Kathy's distrust was hard to swallow. Let's be honest, though… why would she trust me? Based on my words alone, my track record surely didn't warrant immediate trust! My words had to be backed up with consistent action. My actions and reactions had to line up with a new goal in mind…that goal was to move forward and not give up!

The actions that I took to earn Kathy's trust may have seemed radical to others, but they were completely necessary at that time. These were tangible things I did when Kathy and I moved back in together. Here are just a few everyday things that I was intentional about:

- I changed my cell phone number… I had every reason to justify keeping that number, because of my financial responsibility to my family through my martial arts school of nearly 1,000 students.
- I didn't put a password on my phone for years, and once I did, it was a password that Kathy and I shared. She now has all my passwords and access to any device I use. She can look at it anytime with no questions asked.
- My Facebook account is now OUR Facebook account, with the name "Chad Kathy Robichaux."

My life became fully transparent to my wife.

I continue to deliberately maintain that transparency today. Ultimately, I created a security for my wife that will not change. Through the years, these radical changes gained me favor with Kathy and built a level of deep trust that we never had before. We know that, no matter what obstacle we face, we are in our marriage *for a lifetime.* Now, even if insecurity creeps in, Kathy can look deep into my life and ask questions without fear of offending me. This new attitude is not because I don't want to defend myself, but because I care more about defending our marriage instead. Transparency is the key to maintaining trust and unity in marriage, and faith is the key to our relationship with God. These are the keys that have "divorce-proofed" our marriage.

I'm glad I chose to make those radical changes in my everyday living, and I am thankful I persisted in earning Kathy's trust back. I now live with the rewards of that resolve. The pressure of the fear of being exposed, while living in sin, is no longer a lurking cloud over my life…and it feels so great to live in that freedom. I have found the joy in being married to a wife who is content with our marriage and hopeful in its future. Kathy and I are now blessed to be part of a covenant marriage where we are united with a sovereign and loving God who is with us for eternity.

Thank you, God, for a second chance to rebuild trust and faith in my marriage. Thank you that I am now unified with You and my wife, reaping the rewards of living out the marriage You intend for my family.

Proverbs 28:13 (NIV)
13 Whoever conceals their sins does not prosper, but the one who confesses and renounces them finds mercy.

MARRIAGE BUILDER QUESTIONS

1. Do either of you feel insecure in parts of your marriage? What ways can you make your spouse feel more secure?

2. Are there areas in your marriage that need to be more transparent?

3. What radical changes are YOU willing to make to ensure your spouse feels more secure?

Notes

WEEK 20

REBUILDING THE TRUST

...it's never too late

Kathy

I am so thankful that God restored my marriage and brought wonderful mentors like Steve Toth and his wife, Babette, into our lives. Without them, I feel that Chad's willingness to work so hard at our marriage would not have been possible. I know Chad had to exert A LOT of effort, because I was too hurt to make it easy for him. Chad needed many hours of counsel and support that Steve generously offered. He encouraged Chad and enabled him to keep moving forward, even when I was rejecting his efforts.

We had been living apart for nearly three months when I filed for divorce. Chad arrived at his apartment from a getaway with one of his "lady friends" to find that manila envelope sitting at his front door. When he opened the envelope, he realized that I wasn't playing games. Chad was in a bad place on many levels. I'm sure the thought of him losing his family was a sudden reality check for him. I'm not sure why a few pieces of paper jolted him into reality, since the sale of our beautiful home and the pain that our children faced weren't enough to get his attention. I thought, *"How do these documents make it any more real? Does he really think that he can continue his toxic lifestyle and keep me as his wife forever?"* As much as I loved him and had been praying for him, I had lost all hope and was finally ready to walk away from our relationship. Sadly, I had accepted the reality that my husband had moved on with different women and our marriage had come to an end. I bring this up again only because *I want to give you hope!*

> ***We were done! Our home was sold! Divorce papers were filed! Chad was already finding new relationships! One-year contracts were signed on separate apartments! The kids had already been forced into our terrible reality…we couldn't have been closer to the complete collapse of our marriage and the life we had built.***

So, again, PLEASE listen to me closely… No matter how much damage has been done, trust can be rebuilt, hope can be restored, and a marriage you thought impossible could be yours. I believe you need to do whatever it takes to stay together, even if you were not the one who caused that trust to be broken. Chad and I are living proof of the healing power of Jesus Christ! He can make old things new. He can restore the broken-hearted. He can bring your dead marriage back to life. Where trust was once lost, God can bring hope, restoration, joy, and a trust that is greater than the one that was broken. He did that for us, and He can do it for you too. You both have to choose to commit to tap into the plan God has for you; work hard and in time you will find its rewards.

During one of the programs Chad and I do, I get the privilege to speak to men about returning home to their wives and families after the Mighty Oaks Fight Club for Men. I explain how their excitement to rebuild their broken relationships will be difficult. Sadly, I'm the first one to remind them that the problems that they came to Mighty Oaks with are still waiting for them when they return home. A wife who is hurting, bitter, angry, and who no longer has trust in him, may have sent him to our program hopeful for change. However, one thing is for sure…she isn't going to let her guard down just because they come home excited about what they learned. I hate to be the one to burst their bubble, because they make remarkable strides during our sessions. Many of them have made big decisions to go home and take back control of their lives, lead their families, and be the Godly men, husbands, and fathers they were created to be. In fact, most of them are on fire! Yet, we would be doing them an injustice if we sent them home with that motivation, and did not prepare them for the real battle ahead. This is not fun, but I tell them this because I know what it feels like to see my husband say that he is a *new man* and that he is going to do things differently, but then revert back to his old ways. If these wives are like me, they, too, will reject his initial change. The truth is, the very people for whom they will be fighting for will likely fight back, because they will not trust that the change will stick. The fear of being lifted up only to be let down will only raise a higher guard. The insecurity of *"how long will this last before he hurts me again?"* shuts wives down and sends them running the other way. It seems too good to be true… that is exactly where I was when Chad decided he couldn't live without me. The walls went up! The process Chad would endure was not a short one. Before the separation, Chad's way of apologizing was telling me he was sorry, with the expectation of me getting over it, and never bringing it up again. Reassuring me of his love and faithfulness was not a priority to him and never part of his strategy. Chastising me for continuing to bring up his mistakes ended up being the norm. Inside, I was screaming for his love and I wanted so badly to know that *I was the love of his life.* I just didn't know how to communicate that to him. Then it happened…the way he apologized and dealt with my accusations and reminders of the past was not the same as before.

It was not a phase he was going through; he was REALLY a new man.

I'm so proud of my husband and thankful for his love and patience toward me during that time when I rejected his changes. I was not quick to forgive or easy to deal with, but Chad stuck with it anyway…and he did it with love, patience, and grace. This is also a great example of the way God loves us.

The song *Lead Me* [10] by Sanctus Real says it best...

Lead me with strong hands
Stand up when I can't
Don't leave me hungry for love
Chasing dreams, what about us?
Show me you're willing to fight
That I'm still the love of your life
I know we call this our home
But I still feel alone.

Chad was showing me he was "willing to fight." With the help of Steve Toth, Chad was able to put The Lord first in his life. Chad began to pray for us and for me out loud.

When I would start losing hope, Chad would confirm his love for me by holding me in his arms.

He would be vulnerable with me and say how thankful he was to have me. He was truly sorry for the pain he had caused. Chad continually moved forward, no matter how hard it got. He gave me full access to all of his email accounts, and more often than not, he would even leave his phone with me when he would go to the restroom or elsewhere. I was no longer wondering whom he was talking to when he was out of my sight. In the past, if I had ever wanted to see his phone, or look at his email, he would flip out. I knew his changes were radical because this was not the case anymore.

Chad's hard work was paying off, and I realized that if I didn't start accepting his efforts to rebuild my trust, he might walk away for good. I didn't want that to happen because, frankly, I really liked my new and improved husband. Now, I was the one who needed to be nurtured back to health. Healing was taking place in each of us. All in all, it was a solid year before I was able to trust Chad again. In fact, today, I no longer live in fear or insecurity, and

Chad doesn't have to live with my rejection. For the first time in our marriage, I have a husband I completely trust, a marriage I can count on, and the knowledge of a loving God who is always there to bond us together. When the enemy of our soul comes in and tries to tempt me to distrust Chad again, I make the choice to go straight to God. In my weakness, God is my strength. Usually, that one minute it takes to reach out to God saves me hours of fighting with Chad. The enemy tries to steal, kill, and destroy everything Chad and I have worked so hard for. He can't handle the fact that we have made it so far and that we trust and love each other more today than ever before.

Thank you, God, for building a trust into our marriage that has overcome the depths of despair.

> **Joel 2:25 (NIV)**
> *25 "I will repay you for the years the locusts have eaten - the great locust and the young locust, the other locusts and the locust swarm - my great army that I sent among you.*

MARRIAGE BUILDER QUESTIONS

1. *It is a paradox that by giving up our lives, we get them back. As Chad demonstrated, the hidden blessing of purposefully working through our stuff is that we'll never be the same, but better and healthier. What do YOU have to give up to have a better and healthier marriage?*
2. *When we seek to rebuild trust, we may not feel trust or that we are trustworthy, but we can stay committed to try. Discuss your commitment to a covenant marriage.*
3. *Talk about giving your full surrender, intentionality, and persistence to never giving up on your marriage and trusting God to restore "what the locusts have eaten"! Being as specific as possible, what will this look like in your marriage?*

Notes

WEEK 21

LISTEN TO THE "EXTRA" WORDS!

...they count

Chad

One afternoon, on the coast of California, a man was cruising the beach front highway on his Harley Sportster, when all of a sudden a large white cloud appeared overhead, radiating a brilliant light. From that cloud came the powerful, yet peaceful voice that the man immediately knew was God's. The Lord said to the man, "Because you have lived a life of faithfulness, I will grant you one wish while you are still here on earth." The man pulled over to the side of the road. He was amazed, but quickly responded with his heart's desire in that moment. He replied to God, "Will you build me a bridge to Hawaii, so that I can ride over anytime I wish?"

God answered, "Son, your request is worldly, and while I can do all, I want you to think of the enormous challenges that kind of project will entail...the manpower I will have to employ, the pillars necessary to reach the bottom of the Pacific Ocean, and all the concrete and steel that is needed to complete it! I ask that you take time for more thought and consider a wish that would be less selfish and more giving to all mankind."

The man thought deeper and then said, "Lord, I wish on behalf of all men that we could understand women, so that we would know how she feels in her heart, what she's thinking and why she cries at times for no reason. Allow us to understand how to help her when she says nothing is wrong and then snaps and complains when we are only trying to help. Give us the wisdom to clearly communicate our love to her and make her happy."

There was a silence, and then God replied: "Do you want two or four lanes on that bridge?"

Men, I think we can all agree that how to *communicate to* and *understand* women can seem like two of the mysteries of creation. Conversely, women would say the same about our ability to communicate and certainly, our ability to listen. I have read research that says women speak 20,000 words per day, compared to men who speak only 7,000 [10]. That 13,000-word imbalance means we have to be ready to absorb a lot of extra words in order to satisfy our wife's need to communicate to us. So, here is the trick, men…while your wife is rambling, you have to know three simple statements and randomly interject them into your "conversation." In doing so, you will be fine to drift off and think about your upcoming fishing trip next weekend. Here they are: "Interesting!" "How's that make you feel?" and "Tell me more!" If you just follow these simple tips, you'll be well on you way to communicating in a healthy marriage!

Well…MAYBE NOT! Obviously, what I described above is not communication at all. We must care about what our spouses say, because it's part of our marriage union. Our spouses need to be able to share with us. If they can't communicate the struggles, desires, and excitements of life with their spouses, an important need will go unmet. Not meeting a woman's need to *simply be heard* can lead to loneliness, frustration, bitterness and even anger. True communication is not just listening. In fact, it is defined in three parts: talking plus listening plus understanding equals communication. In the past, I didn't think that what Kathy had to say was important enough for me to take the time to listen. I felt that I didn't have the time to hear about what she was thinking. I thought the issues I was dealing with were much more urgent. I just didn't want to take the time to hear about what she was thinking, much less the minute details of it all.

The reality is, this attitude toward communicating with my wife caused the decline in our relationship that took our marriage from that joyful moment when we fell in love to that terrible moment when we fell apart. What happened to take us from that high to that low is called *disassociation*, which is birthed from our inability to communicate our hurt, joy, sadness, or our dreams about the future. We often feel we've expressed those things, but without the *right* form of communication, they will not be fully understood. When we live in a state of disassociation, we can never understand how to fulfill our spouse's needs. I'm talking to both husband and wife now! This is so important to tune into. Even if you learn everything else in this book, yet don't seek to communicate clearly with your spouse, you will encounter continual hardship and you will face constant frustration and the feeling of un-fulfillment in your relationship with your spouse. It is important to know that these feelings of frustration are not entirely your spouse's fault! It's also important to know that these frustrations won't simply go away if you move on to a new relationship. If you don't learn to communicate properly and get divorced over it, you will simply carry your hurt and frustration from one relationship to another and never find the true unity that God intended for your marriage.

> ***Without proper communication, disassociation from love and intimacy will lead to disaffection and isolation.***

Every marriage will experience a natural drift, so you must take a deliberate stance to fight for your marriages and focus on healthy communication.

Today, Kathy and I enjoy a healthy marriage as a direct result of a deliberate focus on communication. For the sake of our marriage and family, we earnestly sought to understand how to effectively communicate our needs, our hurts and our desires. I joked earlier about the extra *13,000 words* that Kathy may need to communicate daily, but she now also understands my need to get information in bite-sized pieces so I can process it better.

> ***We have two very contrasting needs, but we are now both willing to make every effort to meet those needs, which brings us to a point of balance.***

I make myself more available to actually listen to her, and she is willing to not start a "Talk-a-Thon" when she knows I need to idle my mind for a bit. We were able to create this strategy by learning how to communicate our own deepest needs and, at the same time, seeking out and understanding the other's needs as well.

From Biblical counseling to reading books like The *5 Love Languages* [11] by Gary D. Chapman, there are many resources that can assist you in learning about healthy communication and meeting each other's needs. In the list below, there are some needs that you may find your spouse has. Keep in mind, these needs may change as we age, grow, mature, or face hurts and trauma. However, one thing is for sure…your needs are not your spouse's needs, and you will always fall short of trying to treat each other the way *you want to be treated.*

Try this little exercise:

> *Separately and privately write your top three needs on a piece of paper and trade them with one another. Keep your spouse's paper in a place where you will see it daily. Tape it to your bathroom mirror, put it in your wallet, or just some place where you won't forget it. Whether it is verbally, or in action, attempt to meet your spouse's needs on a daily basis. Imagine a marriage where each and every day your spouse met the three greatest needs your heart desired! That isn't a far-off reality if you live this out daily.*

Here are some examples…

Acceptance	Appreciation
Affection	Comfort
Respect	Encouragement
Approval	Freedom
Attention	Security
Support	Receive Gifts
Sexual Fulfillment	Affirmation
Community	Companionship

This project should not seem like a chore. Men, this is not a time to hold hands with your wife and do a "find out her feelings" exercise! Quite the opposite…look at it like this…you are engaging in an exercise that will allow you to both get what you need out of this relationship! The two of you need to agree to ONE RULE… ***Just do it!*** Do your part with a willing and open heart, no matter what has happened in the past or will happen in the future. That means, even if your spouse is not doing their part, keep advancing ahead.

Men, you have to trust me that this is a great exercise that works! I've worked with hundreds of men on this, and believe me… I already know your #1 need, and while I don't need to call it out; I'll just say do your part and you can't lose!

Women, I also already know 9 out of 10 of you will pick "security" as your top need. So, husbands, simply doing this exercise and living out the challenges of this book will already make your wife feel much more secure. Remind her, everyday, that she is your major priority, that there is no Plan B, that you are "all in" and willing to do what it takes to improve your marriage. These words will help to bring her that security she desires. However, the best way to meet your wife's need for security is to pray with her daily! Pray for her on the good days and bad, when you're happy or when you're mad, and continue the fight to be the husband that God called you to be! Pray together with your wife for the wisdom and endurance to align your marriage to be all that God intended it to be.

Throughout this book, we haven't sugarcoated anything. We haven't said it would be easy, and this is especially true when it comes to communication. To tap into the reality of what God's covenant marriage should really look like, you will both need to accept this challenge and become better communicators. As you can imagine, this was the biggest challenge for Kathy and me. I praise God that we discovered the patience, grace, and ultimately the desire to hear and to meet one another's needs. That was the difference that allowed our marriage to survive.

> ***Now, our marriage is not only surviving, but it is thriving with the joy and fulfillment that we've always longed for.***

Praise God for a wife who loves me enough to hear and meet the needs and desires of my heart.

> **Galatians 5:13-15 (NIV)**
> *You, my brothers and sisters, were called to be free. But do not use your freedom to indulge the flesh; rather, serve one another humbly in love. For the entire law is fulfilled in keeping this one command: "Love your neighbor as yourself." If you bite and devour each other, watch out or you will be destroyed by each other.*

MARRIAGE BUILDER QUESTION

Complete the exercise included in this chapter.

Notes

Notes

WEEK 22

FINALLY, SUCCESSFUL COMMUNICATION

Kathy

Successful communication has been a challenge for Chad and me. One thing that I have learned over the years is that if I approach Chad respectfully, my chances of him listening and responding are far greater than if I approach him harshly or aggressively.

For most of our marriage, Chad has had no desire to take out the trash. It could be packed tight, overflowing, and causing a seriously foul smell throughout our home, and he still wouldn't think about taking it out. That drives me crazy! I know he isn't lazy; in fact, he is one of the hardest workers I know. What makes me crazy is that I feel he takes me for granted because he knows that I have all the home chores covered.

Here are two ways that I could deal with this:

A. I could communicate what I desire to have done by asking him respectfully *"Honey, can you please take out the trash?"*

OR

B. I could express my frustration to him with my finger pointed by disrespectfully saying, *"You never do anything, the trash smells like a dead pig! When do you plan on taking that out?"*

A gentle answer turns away wrath, but a harsh word stirs up anger. (Proverbs 15:1)

Those who guard their mouths and their tongues keep themselves from calamity. (Proverbs 13:3)

As a woman of God, I know that I am called to respect my husband. In fact, in last week's lesson, Chad spoke about the needs of our spouses. One of Chad's top three needs is "respect." If I want him to meet my needs, I must first try to meet his needs, even if he is not doing something the way I think he should. It is pretty obvious that Option A would be the best way to handle this situation, but showing Chad respect is not always easy for me. I really struggle with showing him respect when I am frustrated. Truthfully there are many times that I want to go "cuckoo" on him and use Option B (and sadly, I have). However, it never works out well! By using Option B, maybe the trash will get taken out, but the whole day would be ruined because of our anger and fighting. Division would come between us, and what could have been a good day would become filled with chaos. Unfortunately, I have caused one too many "bad days" by not choosing to honor The Lord by respecting my husband. Taking the approach of choosing to honor The Lord is exactly how I started to make the appropriate changes in my attitude. Ephesians 5 teaches us to respect our husbands. That verse doesn't say to respect him *only when he deserves it.* Instead, God's Word teaches us to respect our husbands *all of the time.* It was with this new revelation in mind that I was able to begin making the choice to respect Chad in all areas of our marriage, *but especially with my words.*

I was convicted by these verses in the Bible:

> *Better to live in a desert than with a quarrelsome and nagging wife.* (Proverbs 21:19)
>
> *Better to live on a corner of the roof than share a house with a quarrelsome wife.* (Proverbs 21:9)

I never want to be that kind of wife again. How shameful it would be if I were still that type of wife?

> *Rather, it should be that of your inner self, the unfading beauty of a gentle and quiet spirit, which is of great worth in God's sight.* (1Peter 3:4)

I made the decision that this is the wife I wanted to be!

This is an example of true beauty. This is the depiction of the virtuous woman that God created me to be. This is the woman who will lay pride aside to willfully meet her husband's needs. Ultimately, this healthy attitude will lead to joy in a marriage that revolves around peace and unity.

After reading the above statement, I'm sure you're asking, "That all sounds wonderful, but if we are so focused on our spouse's needs, then what about our own needs?" Notice what I said above: "the woman who will lay pride aside to willfully meet her husband's needs finds joy in a marriage of peace and unity." There is no question that I still desire to have my needs met, but constantly challenging my husband to meet those needs is selfish on my part, and my efforts always fail. Through true servanthood to one another, when I strive to meet his needs and he strives to meet mine, we find ourselves in the marriage we both desire. I have heard it said that you have to meet halfway…I no longer believe this to be true. I'm willing to go all the way! Even if Chad only goes 30%, then we will be fine, because there will be other days when he will give 100% and I will fall short. You don't have to be a statistician, just understand that when you are both "all in" and can take your eyes off your own needs and focus on your spouse's needs, you will be most fulfilled.

However, this utopia requires you to communicate your needs. You have to be able to say what you are thinking and how things make you feel. Last week, Chad gave you an exercise that focused on communication of needs. Here is another way to express your needs without being an emotional "drama queen!" (Your husband will just tune out your drama anyway...just saying!)

It goes like this…

> "When you do ____________________
>
> …. it makes me feel like ____________".

This may seem silly, and men, you may think there's no way you're saying this scripted line when you're mad, but trust me, *you can do it!* Chad does it all the time! Believe me, we work with some pretty tough dudes, and if they can successfully use this exercise, so can YOU.

Imagine the difference and the clarity of communication between these two statements:

A. "You always go to bed without saying goodnight, you don't even care anymore, and you probably are thinking about being with someone else. I hate this marriage and don't even know why we are together anymore."

OR

B. "When you *go to bed without saying goodnight*, it makes me feel *insecure and unloved.*"

Option A expresses anger and frustration and in no way communicates how you are truly feeling or prompts a change: in reality, it simply picks a fight. Option B, however, clearly communicates the problem and how it makes you feel. It is a fair statement that requires thought and evaluating responsibility to effect change. In short, it's productive communication that will go somewhere. Learning how to communicate this way shows one another that you are trying to move forward. For Chad and me, just knowing the other was trying went a long way.

When Chad and I moved back in together, we knew that we needed to change the way we communicated our needs. We knew that nothing was going to change if we didn't take drastic steps to do so. Our old ways didn't work. Because I was so insecure and worried about what Chad was doing, or whom he was talking to every time he was on his phone and would walk away from me, fear would overtake me. I knew that if I were to ever move forward with Chad, I needed security in this area. There was no way that my marriage would have been able to pull through the infidelity successfully, nor would I ever be able feel secure in my marriage if Chad were not willing to go out of his way to show me his faithfulness. I had to use the above exercise and constantly say, *"when you…I feel."* I felt a little silly at first, but this tool helped us so much. For example, I would say, *"Chad, when you walk away from me on your phone while you're texting, it makes me feel fearful and insecure that you may be talking to another woman."*

Wow, how easy, clear and direct was that? After I expressed my emotional need of security by using the exercise, Chad actually knew what my hurt was and took responsibility and action to correct it, no fight needed. The best thing about this new strategy was that it was Chad's choice and desire to give me the security I longed for. I didn't have to make him do it. Chad has come very far in his ability to meet my emotional needs. Because he has done so well, I now have no fear or worry about whom Chad is speaking to or texting out of my sight. I never thought there would be hope for restoration in this area.

Thank you, God, for giving Chad the willingness to love me enough to go out of his way to give me security.

1 Peter 3:4 (NIV)
4 Rather, it should be that of your inner self, the unfading beauty of a gentle and quiet spirit, which is of great worth in God's sight.

MARRIAGE BUILDER QUESTIONS

Do you ever feel that you're in a vicious cycle that is never ending? It feels like there is no hope? Praise The Lord, it does not have to stay that way. You can reverse it and make that vicious cycle a victorious circle. How are you going to choose today to effectively communicate with your spouse? Do you want to see victory? Choose today that you are going to honor The Lord first, seek to meet your spouse's needs, and be deliberate in effectively communicating your needs, hurts, and desires to your spouse. The marriage you desire is only a few choices away, and rest assured that God will honor those choices. You will experience joy, peace, and unity where you never thought they were possible.

Use the exercise in this chapter and discuss your new communication tactics.

Notes

Notes

WEEK 23

THE COVENANT MARRIAGE

...the way He intended it

Chad & Kathy

Throughout this book, you've heard us talk about "God's plan" for your marriage, or "the covenant marriage." We've called this connection many things, but this week, we'd like to dig into what God's design for your marriage looks like and why it works.

Have you ever gone to a furniture store and bought a self-assembly product, maybe an entertainment center or a kitchen table? If you're like us, you open the box and remove all the contents, like blocks of wood, plastic parts, and various bags of nuts and bolts. You take a look at the picture on the outside of the box and think, *"No problem, I got this!"* Oh, there is that little paper booklet that comes with it...the instruction manual. You just toss that aside for now, because you clearly see the parts and the picture of the final product. So, what could go wrong? A few frustrating hours and maybe even a few un-choice words later, you have something that resembles the product in that picture, but with maybe a few "extra" parts. We typically say, "Those "extra" parts are in case something breaks, or maybe someone at the factory made a mistake, but certainly not us!"

What is it about us that we won't take time to read the instruction manual? Are we too prideful and arrogant, or too lazy to invest the time into doing it right? Either way, the final product is never what it was intended to be, and when the legs fall off the table because they can't hold the weight of Thanksgiving dinner, we are either surprised or upset. Instead of looking at the one who was responsible for following the directions that were clearly laid out, we often blame the product for somehow being cheap or flawed.

In case you're not tracking with this example, we are making a clear parallel to our marriages. Why are we so quick to jump into marriage without taking the time to read the blueprints, follow the instruction manual, and understand what God's plan has been for our marriage all along? It's because we look at a picture of marriage and say, "I can do that!" The problem is, most of those "pictures" and examples we will see of marriages represented around us are flawed. Even the most picture-perfect marriages will face the struggles of this world and living life together. When the hardships come and life spins our marriage sideways, we should always go back to the original source: *the perfect set of instructions God provided for us.* When we don't, and the weight and pressure of life comes on us, the legs blow out and we begin to say to ourselves that somehow the marriage was bad, or one spouse is to blame…that we aren't compatible, or we grew apart! The truth is, when you don't follow the instructions for a marriage, then you are to blame. We are talking to both husband and wives. *You need to take responsibility to learn and understand what God's plan is for your marriage.*

The good news with God is, it is not too late.

God's plan for your marriage may not have been something you've considered in the past, but the beauty about making the choice to change the path of your marriage and to calibrate your marriage to His plan is that living the covenant marriage heals the old and births the new. It may not seem possible now, but we are telling you that *we are living testimonies of this transformation!* Every day, we're blessed to experience our marriage as God intended it. The more healing we experience from our past hurts, the more those hurts seem like a distant memory, rather than part of our current reality. We have found healing, forgiveness, peace, true joy, and fulfillment through what we call the covenant marriage. All you need to do is to read the instruction manual to enjoy a marriage the way God intended it to be.

To help you get started, we wanted to share a little overview... some of the basics and highlights of this *covenant marriage.* First, I think it is important to recognize that in the Bible, in the book of Genesis, God creates male and female to be together, illustrating the marriage covenant bonded by Him to be the very first institution He created.

Genesis 2:18–25 (NIV)
The Lord God said, "It is not good for the man to be alone. I will make a helper suitable for him."

Now The Lord God had formed out of the ground all the wild animals and all the birds in the sky. He brought them to the man to see what he would name them; and whatever the man called each living creature, that was its name. So the man gave names to all the livestock, the birds in the sky and all the wild animals.

But for Adam no suitable helper was found. So The Lord God caused the man to fall into a deep sleep; and while he was sleeping, he took one of the man's ribs and then closed up the place with flesh. Then The Lord God made a woman from the rib he had taken out of the man, and he brought her to the man.

The man said, "This is now bone of my bones and flesh of my flesh; she shall be called 'woman,' for she was taken out of man." That is why a man leaves his father and mother and is united to his wife, and they become one flesh.
Adam and his wife were both naked, and they felt no shame.

As with many scriptures in the Bible, we tend to read through the content and not completely grasp the message. Adam said, *"This is now bone of my bones and flesh of my flesh; she shall be called 'woman,' for she was taken out of man. That is why a man leaves his father and mother and is united to his wife, and they become one flesh."* God gave Adam a wife, and Adam communicates their ONENESS. This is both a beautiful and powerful part of scripture and the foundational principle of marriage. It is the introduction of a tri-union relationship between a man and a woman, united by their God. This oneness brings you to the position that we've shared throughout this book: You are not completed by one another; rather, you are united together as one to face the challenges of this world. This is the way marriage was meant to be. This is the recipe for success for a marriage that will stand the test of time and bring the joy and fulfillment that you both desire. It starts with a personal relationship with Christ and the unification of your marriage under God.

Aligning your marriage with God's plan doesn't mean you won't face hardships...*you will.* This world and the devil that dwells in it will throw everything at you to destroy your marriage. The ultimate goal of your covenant marriage is that during those hardships, you must stay unified and conquer them as one. There will be some failures along the way, but keep in mind that those failures *do not define your marriage, but they refine it* as you make adjustments and recalibrate to God's plan. There's a big difference between those two things, and recognizing that difference will save you some frustration and loss of hope.

As we've mentioned in previous chapters, *God never intended for you to be divorced.* Biblically, marriage is defined as a solemn and binding relationship to last a LIFETIME. I love the conversation Jesus has with the Pharisees who were opposing Him on the subject of divorce:

Matthew 19:3–9 (NIV)
Pharisees: Some Pharisees came to Him (Jesus) to test him.

> *They asked, "Is it lawful for a man to divorce his wife for any and every reason?"*
>
> *Jesus: "Haven't you read," He replied, "that at the beginning the Creator 'made them male and female,' and said, 'For this reason a man will leave his father and mother and be united to his wife, and the two will become one flesh'? So they are no longer two, but one flesh. Therefore what God has joined together, let no one separate."*
>
> *Pharisees: "Why then," they asked, "did Moses command that a man give his wife a certificate of divorce and send her away?"*
>
> *Jesus: "Moses permitted you to divorce your wives because your hearts were hard. But it was not this way from the beginning.*

Jesus' words are powerful and permanent, yet too often we consider them only relevant to our personal circumstances…as if somehow the rules don't apply to us, because no one could ever understand how bad we have it. Jesus' words really impacted us as we began to understand this oneness covenant marriage, *"So they are no longer two, but one flesh. Therefore what God has joined together, let no one separate."*

The Pharisees, like us, tried to justify divorce because of the world around them. As the Pharisees asked Jesus, *"Why then, did Moses command that a man give his wife a certificate of divorce and send her away?"* His answer is crushing: *"Moses permitted you to divorce your wives because your hearts were hard. But it was not this way from the beginning."* What Jesus is saying here is that Moses made a concession for divorce because people wouldn't do it God's way. Couples simply didn't choose to seek God's plan and had hardened their hearts toward one another. Out of selfish agendas and hardened hearts, man created divorce, but it is not part of God's plan.

Thank you, God, for a perfect plan and instruction for our marriage, and for the wisdom and clarity to seek Your Word in order to align our marriage to be the covenant marriage you intended from the beginning.

Matthew 19:6 (NIV)
6 So they are no longer two, but one flesh. Therefore what God has joined together, let no one separate."

MARRIAGE BUILDER QUESTIONS

1. *Read the following verses out loud together and then discuss the Biblical road map for marriage:*
   Genesis 2:22–24
   Proverbs 5:18–19
   Proverbs 19:14
   Proverbs 20:6–7
   Proverbs 30:18–19
   Ephesians 5:22–33
   1 Corinthians 7:1–16
   Hebrews 13:4–7
   Mark 10:6–9
2. *God does have a plan for your marriage. He desires to see your love grow and bear fruit. The goal of a covenant marriage is not to merely enjoy each other's company nor is it to simply endure to the end. The goal of a covenant marriage is to glorify God in your relationship and to exemplify Christ to the world.*

   Discuss how your marriage will glorify God and exemplify Christ in the future.

Notes

Notes

WEEK 24

SERVANT LEADERSHIP

Chad

Through my years of being deployed in Afghanistan, the traditional roles in our family became blurred. Our marriage roles at that time were necessary to keep the family together and moving forward through life. Kathy never called me in Afghanistan to tell me the washing machine wasn't working or to complain that she had ten destinations for the kids on her most stressful days, because she knew I couldn't do anything about it anyway. I think she always viewed her role as a warrior's wife that could hold things together when I was away. It was comforting to know my home and children were in good hands. In retrospect, Kathy carried most of the responsibility for our family during those years. She was the most amazing mom, but she also filled the void as "dad"… she was an amazing wife, but she also filled in for the duties as "husband." She did it all and didn't complain, because she knew I needed that support to do my job; for a season, it worked for us. However, when I came home for good and struggled with the frustration of being diagnosed with PTSD, I never seemed to be able to clearly redefine our marriage roles. Even if you know those marriage roles, as the Bible would define them, that doesn't make it always easy to live them out…especially when you have become accustomed to living life a certain way. Military wives often rise up, just like Kathy did, to take the reins, and then their husbands come home and try to take them back. Often, those men don't maintain that leadership role in a consistent manner and only play the part when it's convenient for them to do so. When men don't rise up in ALL areas of the Biblical responsibility to lead, women tend to fill in the void and rise to the occasion. Ultimately, "Momma-Bear moms" end up taking control over the family. Usually a fight for control will ensue. This fight can turn into chaos in the home.

Often, when I challenge men to take charge in their homes, they tell me it won't work for their marriages. They tell me that I wouldn't understand because their wives aren't like mine and that they are married to dominant women. My response may sting, but fellas, it's true. I say, "If you show me a dominant woman, I'll show you a weak man."

> ***A man who is not leading his family will prompt his wife to step up and fill the void.***

This displacement of roles always leads to conflict between the husband and wife.

So what does it mean to lead? Does it mean men are domineering, somehow superior or in charge? The Bible clearly states that men and women are equal, but it also states that husbands and wives have different roles. The interpretation of these roles is one of the most controversial and misused perspectives of a Biblical marriage. If you don't get them right in your marriage, you will constantly be working against the grain. In fact, I would say that beyond a triune relationship between a man, a woman, and their God, following the Biblical roles for marriage are the foundational keys to success.

Here it comes...the role of the husband is HEAD! Ephesians 5:23 says, *"For the husband is the head of the wife as Christ is the head of the church, his body, of which he is the Savior. Now as the church submits to Christ, so also wives should submit to their husbands in everything. Husbands, love your wives, just as Christ loved the church and gave himself up for her."*

Some men might extract *"husband is the head"* and *"wives should submit"*...but let's look deeper into understanding this in its entirety. The model for a husband's role with his wife is given to us through Jesus Christ and His relationship to the church. Jesus' example is that of a servant that is *humbling himself.* There is not a more perfect example of servant leadership than the life of Jesus Christ! Was Jesus head of the Church? Yes, but He gave himself up for her; He died for the Church, for us. I often hear men talk in an attempt at chivalry and say, "I'd die for my wife!!! But, when it comes to taking out the trash, that is where I draw the line!" To what lengths are you willing to go as the servant leader of your marriage? Jesus showed us that there are no limits of servanthood, as He gave His life for us in the most brutal way.

I get the opportunity to teach this principle to military men through our ministry, and ironically, even with a military divorce rate of over 80%, this model of servant leadership makes sense to them. I explain it like this...you're in an infantry platoon in Afghanistan and as you finish your day's patrol, you stop to establish an objective rally point to conduct your mission. As orders are being tasked out, the officer in charge, the "head," decides he's going to kick his feet up while the troops dig in some defensive positions. In fact, why don't you get the "boss-man" a cup of coffee before you start digging in those rocks? Who would follow this guy? We would all follow the leader who is right there, shoulder to shoulder, busting rocks and pulling his weight, getting dirty and leading by example. In fact, these are the leaders whom men will follow and for whom they would die for.

That is the type of leadership we all understand! So, why do we walk in our homes after a hard day's work and somehow think that we are entitled to be "the head man" of the house? What real leaders understand about being "the head" is that ultimately, we are RESPONSIBLE. *Taking responsibility for everyone under our authority, including ourselves, is true leadership.*

So when my fifteen-year-old sneaks out of the house at 1AM to go to a party, do I address it and discipline him? Absolutely! However, as the leader, I also look at myself and evaluate where my fault in that situation lies, and how I can improve as a leader.

Now, everyone who knows a little about the military knows that the officer in charge, whether he be the "feet-up-coffee-lover," or the "grungy leader" who gets in the dirt with his men, will have a "number two" leader. The crazy thing about the "number two's" in the military is that they are typically the most experienced. That new lieutenant, fresh out of college and Officer Candidate School, is pretty motivated to lead with all his academic knowledge. On the other hand, the "number two" in his command, right under him, is an old crusty staff sergeant who doesn't care much about the books this college kid read. In fact, the greatest knowledge many young lieutenants will gain will be from the platoon sergeant they were first in charge of. The military does a brilliant job of creating a balance of authority and wisdom, brought together in unity to form a unit capable of success and growth.

In the marriage, we see the same model. The man is the authority, but the "number two" is the wife, "the helper," as a source of knowledge, intuition, and, often, the patience and humility to hear God. It is a perfect and beautiful unit designed for success and growth. In Genesis 2:18, God says, *"It is not good for the man to be alone. I will make a helper suitable for him."* Ephesians 5:24 tells us, *"Now as the church submits to Christ, so also wives should submit to their husbands in everything."* But don't jump for joy just yet, men…leaders are willing to cut their teeth in the trenches and earn the respect and trust of those whom they are called to serve. I believe that this model is the God-given desire of both a man and woman's heart.

The process starts with men taking their roles as servant leaders, humbling themselves and accepting responsibility for their own faults, as well as the faults of those entrusted to them by God. In doing this in my own marriage, while having also witnessed other men take the lead in filling their own Biblical role in a marriage covenant, I have witnessed families restored. I have seen dominant wives find joy and relief from no longer having to carry a burden and weight they were never meant to carry. I have seen children grow in their faith as Biblical roles of Godly leadership are modeled in their homes. When men of God humble themselves, take responsibility, and fully submit to God's leadership, *The Lord restores their families, and their wives and children become willing to follow and trust their leadership.*

Mark 10:45 (NIV)
45 For even the Son of Man did not come to be served, but to serve, and to give his life as a ransom for many."

MARRIAGE BUILDER QUESTIONS

1. *Servant leadership is best defined by Jesus Himself: "Whoever wants to become great among you must be your servant, and whoever wants to be first must be your slave—just as the Son of Man did not come to be served, but to serve, and to give his life as a ransom for many" (Matthew 20:26–28). In the Christian realm, all leadership should be servant leadership.*

   Discuss the type of leadership you have seen modeled in your life.

2. *As Chad shared his military example of the "head man" and his "number two," discuss how this might work practically in your marriage.*

3. *What commitments are you willing to make to adjust your marriage to exemplify appropriate Biblical roles?*

NOTES

Week 25

The Legacy of Marriage

Pastor Jeremy Stalnecker

Today, I had the privilege of participating in the Marriage Vow Renewal for Chad and Kathy's twentieth wedding anniversary. They have been planning this renewal as a way to recommit themselves to each other and to the vows that they made when they entered into this covenant relationship as young adults. Although I am sure that the last twenty years have had far more struggles than they ever anticipated, they have allowed God to work through those difficulties to strengthen their own marriage and now to strengthen the marriages of many others. As I reflect on the ceremony and what this day means to them, I am reminded of the amazing legacy that a couple will leave if they remain committed to a marriage built on the foundation of Christ.

Our legacy is what we will leave behind to the generation coming behind us. It is the birthright, or heritage, of those that we have been given the responsibility to lead. When I think about the legacy left by a couple committed to Christ, I first think about how important this relationship is to God Himself. When God decided to leave on earth a legacy of His great love for us, He chose to use the marriage relationship. We are told that the husband and wife are to reflect the relationship of Christ and His bride, the Church. Literally, when someone looks at a couple devoted to one another and committed to the model of marriage outlined in Scripture, they should see in real time a picture of the legacy of love, sacrifice, and provision that God has given us. Our birthright as Christians is reflected in this relationship when a man and woman are living in a loving, sacrificial relationship with one another. How amazing that God would choose to use two imperfect people committed to each other and to Him, as His example of love for us!

Understanding that God has designed the marriage relationship as a picture of His legacy, I cannot help but believe that it is also part of His design that marriages would not only last but would thrive. We are not perfect, but our Designer has made it possible for us to enjoy a relationship that is personally fulfilling while at the same time allows us to show others the way forward. Our legacy as married people should be one that reflects and points our children and others toward God's truth. Unfortunately, this is often not the case. The legacy that many couples will leave for their children and others coming up behind them is one of anger, frustration, and brokenness. Instead of pointing others to the hope found in a loving, sacrificial relationship with Christ, a picture is painted that portrays uncertainty and fear. What is handed down in this case to those who are looking for direction is an example of failure that removes any hope of success. Children raised in a volatile or broken home believe that this is "just the way it is," and expect the same from their own relationships.

> ***Brokenness becomes a generational problem as each generation builds upon the legacy of brokenness that they inherit.***

The good news is that it does not have to be this way! God created marriage and designed it to leave the right kind of legacy that will impact generations to do great things resulting in hope-filled, love-infused, secure relationships of their own. What we must remember, however, is that leaving a legacy that is worth handing down to those coming behind us will not just happen. If we are going to point our children and others in need of a clear direction forward, it will only be when we first decide to live with the end in mind. We need to live each day of our lives asking the simple question: "If it all ended today, how would I be remembered, and what would I leave behind?" A very simple clarifying question for married couples is this: "If my children grew up to become the same kind of husband or wife as me, what would their marriage look like?" That is what legacy is all about. It is about building a life that, if emulated, would lead to success! It is about living every day for something bigger than yourself and understanding that you are a picture of Christ's love, pointing others to Him.

The amazing thing about living with the end in mind is that if we are living to leave the right kind of legacy, we will not only build a life worth following but will build a life worth living! As we live with the end in mind, we are building a life and a marriage that will be personally fulfilling because it will align with God's plan. This is one of the amazing things to me about God. When we live according to our design, we please Him, bless others, and enjoy the life that He has provided. Marriage is at times extremely difficult, and bringing two broken people together is not easy. If done according to the principles found in Scripture, it will be a blessing to generations of families.

One thing that I have learned about people is that even when they have the best of intentions they will, from time to time, get off track. Over the years I have officiated and attended many weddings. Interestingly, I have never spoken to a couple before the vows were exchanged where they expressed to me the heartache that they were looking forward to in their married life together. In fact, I have tried to warn a few couples of some things that I thought may be problems, but in every case they said that I was wrong. When a couple is looking forward to building a life together, they typically have every intention of keeping their vows and enjoying every minute of "wedded bliss." As we know, though, it does not always work out that way. In fact, even in the very best marriages there are moments when the husband and wife wonder if life may not be better apart. Something that must be remembered is that as long as you are married, your opportunity to build a legacy of hope and encouragement has not passed!

There are those who think they have gone too far or caused too much damage to ever leave anything of value. Others have their own history of broken relationships and are convinced that they will never be able to have anything better. Thankfully, the grace of God is bigger than our failures. If we will begin to live according to His plan, we can begin to build the marriage we were created for, regardless of our past.

This is what makes today's Marriage Vow Renewal so special. One of the things that I have always appreciated about Chad and Kathy is how honest they are about their own marriage journey. This book, in fact, allows them to honestly tell the story of their own trials so that others can be helped. And even with the many struggles that they have experienced over twenty years of marriage, they stood today and recommitted their love for each other, their love for God, and their desire to have the marriage that God intended.

> ***A Marriage Vow Renewal is nothing more than two imperfect people acknowledging that although they have not done everything right, they are going to continue to live and work to leave a legacy that provides hope and points others to Christ.***

It is a wonderful expression of God's grace when we fall, and then rely upon His strength to get up and continue moving toward the life that He created us to live. By renewing their vows, Chad and Kathy are not saying that the past did not happen or that the future will always be bright. They are acknowledging that in spite of the past and the hardships to come, they will live for Christ and build a legacy that blesses the future generations of their family.

Perhaps you have seen your own marriage in the pages of this book. While I am thankful for the Robichaux's willingness to share their difficulties with the rest of us, I am confident that their story is not unique. This book is not about having the perfect marriage or living a life free from conflict. It is about realizing that there is a reason to follow God's plan for marriage that is bigger than any one person.

> ***It is about realizing that the decisions you make today will impact not only you, but your children and the generations of children to come.***

Will you decide to live with the end in mind? Will you decide to align your marriage to God's plan? Will you decide to leave a legacy behind that will show the way forward for those looking for direction? How amazing to know that we can reflect Christ's love and provide hope by living the life God has created for us.

> **Matthew 19:4-6 (NIV)**
> *4 "Haven't you read," He replied, "that at the beginning the Creator 'made them male and female,' 5 and said, 'For this reason a man will leave his father and mother and be united to his wife, and the two will become one flesh'? 6 So they are no longer two, but one flesh. Therefore what God has joined together, let no one separate."*

MARRIAGE BUILDER QUESTIONS

1. *We will all leave a legacy —negative, positive or so-so. What will yours be? What kind of world are you creating around you for others (especially your spouse and children)? What kind of a legacy are you living out for your children to see and to follow?*

2. *If your children, or those around you, were asked if they would want a marriage like yours, would they say "yes"? Can those around you truly look at you as a person of integrity —a living example of someone who reflects the love and character of Christ? THAT is a legacy worth living!*

Think and pray about it. Today can be a new beginning for how you live out your life and the legacy you leave behind. We hope you will make it a goal to live your legacy as one of a spouse who contributed good, and not harm, to your marriage. We pray that thousands of you will leave behind a legacy of a good marriage, to the glory of God.

Notes

Notes

WEEK 26

PAYING IT FORWARD

...it's bigger than yourself!

Chad

The restoration of our marriage was not just accomplished for our enjoyment, as it is also to be used as an illustration of God's love and grace. We have opened our hearts and lives to share His story with you in the hope that this book will bring you the same healing and restoration we have discovered for our marriage. We believe that if you follow the suggestions in this book and are intentional and deliberate about doing the work needed, you will also enjoy a second chance to enjoy God's perfect plan for YOUR marriage.

However, the question then will be, what do I do next? First of all, you will always face struggles while on this earth...*in life and in marriage.* Once you calibrate your marriage to God's plan, you will have to continue to recalibrate it as satan and the world around you attempt to tear it apart. Stay the course and know the victory has already been won, so long as you are seeking Him.

There is more beyond your own victory.

Victory in Christ is not about you. It's also not about your Marriage. It's about God's Kingdom! In the work we do with our military warriors at Mighty Oaks, one of the first things we tell them is, "You think you came here to get well, but that is not the reason you are here. You are here to get well for the purpose of positioning yourself to help the next guy." That is Christ's story; that is our story...*we must pay it forward.* Paying it forward gives us purpose and accountability and ensures that we continue to grow. The simplest way to pay it forward is to simply share what God has revealed to you, where you are and where you are going.

If I were diagnosed with terminal cancer and then found the cure, I couldn't help but want to share it. My new lease on life would be exhilarating, and the knowledge of this new and unknown cure would be information I couldn't keep to myself. I would be compelled, in fact, I would feel obligated, to shout from the rooftops "cancer has been defeated and can no longer take human life if you simply utilize the cure!"

That is how Kathy and I feel about God's restorative power and covenant plan for marriage! *We can't help but share it.* We now have a new lease on life, and it is exhilarating and joyful. The source of the knowledge is something we cannot contain, and that is the purpose of this book. Kathy and I often get asked how we can continue to share and be so transparent about our story. First, it glorifies God, as we show where we came from and where He has brought us to now. Second, we feel we've come so far from the marriage we had to where we are today that it seems as if we are speaking about a totally different couple. Finally, we cannot help but think about the marriages that ended in divorce in the past and those that are facing their demise now. If only couples could know about the cure, the truth, the hope, and the restoration God has for them.

How can we NOT share our story? We feel compelled, obligated, and led by God to use the very thing that almost destroyed us to minister to others. In Genesis 50:20, after Joseph's brothers had perpetrated wrongs against him, he told them that what they meant for evil, God intended for good. This same story played out in our lives. The destruction the enemy had planned for us was redirected by God to be used for His good. We have been blessed to see others inspired and then find hope and restoration in Christ through the story that God has written through our marriage. So when we get to speak in churches, marriage conferences, one on one, and through this book, we will shout it from the rooftops that the cancer that destroys marriages has been defeated! If we tap into this cure through a life and relationship with Jesus Christ and live the life He has created for us, satan can no longer destroy life, love, and the joy God intended for marriage.

It is our challenge for each of you to PAY IT FORWARD; we did not keep this cure a secret when we received it. We have and will continue to share it and so should you. Pass this book on, or help another couple through it. One of the greatest gifts in the Christian walk is mentorship and sharing His truth and encouraging others to do the same. That is the model of discipleship, leading others to continue to mentor and pass on truth and wisdom. Don't let this gift end with you!

To be qualified, you don't have to have it all figured out, or have all the answers…you just have to use your own testimony to *point others to The One who does have all the answers.* Always remember that your testimony is not about what you are doing but what Christ did at the cross for you!

He qualifies us all.

Romans 8:28 (NIV)
28 And we know that in all things God works for the good of those who love him, who have been called according to his purpose.

MARRIAGE BUILDER QUESTIONS

1. *What will you do with your story as God unveils the victory and purpose in your marriage?*

2. *Name three couples with whom you can share this book.*
    a. *As a couple, start praying for them.*

    b. *As a couple, develop a plan to share this book or your story with those couples.*

    c. *As a couple, follow through with seeing these couples into the marriage that God has for them.*

    **Consider leading other couples through this 26-week book. You can also purchase additional copies at: www.MarriageAdvance.org*

Notes

Notes

AFTERWORD

Honorable Steve & Babette Toth
Texas State Legislator

One of the greatest life blessings for Babette and I has been our friendship with Chad and Kathy Robichaux. Jesus said, *"He has sent me to proclaim freedom for the prisoners and recovery of sight for the blind, to set the oppressed free"* (Luke 4:18).

As I explain Chad and Kathy's ministry of Mighty Oaks, I tell people that when our young men come home from Iraq or Afghanistan, as soon as they get off the plane, they immediately lose four things:

- Cohesion
- Sense of mission
- Sense of purpose
- A Job

As soon at they step foot on U.S. soil, many of them are broken and are emotionally and spiritually in critical condition. While they may not know it at the time, their greatest need isn't regaining the four things they lost when they stepped off the plane. Their greatest need is finding that which they never had.

All the destructive things Chad used to fill that empty place in his heart were a cheap substitute for what his heart was longing for. As Babette and I walked with them through their hurt and pain, we waited, loved, and prayed for them both to come to the realization that they needed to go deeper with The Lord than what a stale religion could provide. King David said, *"Taste and see that The Lord is good; blessed is the one who takes refuge in Him"* (Psalms 34:8).

Trying to describe God's goodness is like trying to describe what a fine Texas rib-eye tastes like. You just can't do it. God waits and longs for us to taste, see, and experience His goodness. The Lord's goodness is abundantly evident in the life of the Robichaux family today. Babette and I witnessed their difficult journey and how God was faithful through it all.

In all the years of walking with people who's marriages were in distress, no couple has shown more obedience to Christ and courage to face their issues as Chad and Kathy. While a great foundation for marriage is built on obedience to Jesus in all things, it's reinforced with John the Baptist's confession of faith in where he says:

"He [Jesus] must increase and I must decrease" (John 3:30).

I really don't know who Chad Robichaux was when I met him. Frankly, I don't remember much about him. That Chad is dead and gone. Kathy Robichaux, who was a bottomless pit of hurt and despair, is gone as well. Today, I would like to say I see a couple, but it's more accurate to depict them as a "holy union" set apart for a special purpose. They are making an eternal difference in the lives of everyone they touch.

As exciting as their story may be, it's a story that is available for you as well because it's not based on what they brought to God. It's based on His faithfulness to give rest to all who would come to Him.

We love you, Chad and Kathy.

Steve & Babette

Kathy, Steve and Chad

About the Authors

Chad and Kathy

Chad and Kathy have been married for twenty years and have three teenage children: Hunter, Haili, and Hayden. Chad served eight tours in the Afghanistan War on Terror. After four years of deployments, their family spent years recovering from PTSD and shares a story from tragedy to triumph in their victory of the struggles our warriors face in returning home. They now dedicate their lives to share their story of victory through Christ and to mentor to others like them.

Chad M. Robichaux, BCPC

Chad is the vice president of Serving California over Veteran Affairs and the founder of the Mighty Oaks Warrior Programs (a 501c3 non-profit effort). Chad and his team are dedicated to helping America's military warriors and their families who are suffering from the "unseen wounds" of combat such as PTSD. Their efforts are aimed at developing and implementing interventions with the ultimate goal of reducing the veteran suicide rate and the astronomical divorce rate among veterans.
In addition to being an ordained pastor, Chad is a board-certified pastoral counselor with the Board Certified Professional and Pastoral Counselors and the American Association of Christian Counselors. He specializes in PTSD, trauma care, marriage, and family. Chad earned a Ph.D. in international business management and an M.B.A. from New York Tech, and is a best-selling author with his book *Redeployed*, ranked #1 on the Amazon Best Seller List.

In addition to Chad's military service as a Special Operations Force Recon Marine, he has served our nation as a Federal Special Agent with the U.S. Federal Air Marshal Service, operated for the Department of Defense Special Operations Command (SOCOM), and was a Senior Program Manager for the U.S. State Department in the elite International Surveillance Detection Program. Chad received the Medal of Valor for his bravery beyond the call of duty in law enforcement.

Chad is also a professional athlete with NBC's *World Series of Fighting* and a former MMA World Champion who has used his platform to advocate the civilian support of America's warriors returning home. In addition to *World Series of Fighting*, Chad has competed in Showtime's *StrikeForce*, MTV2's *Bellator FC*, and *Legacy FC* on HDNet and AXStv.

Kathy R. Robichaux

Kathy is the director of Women's Programs and co-founder of Mighty Oaks Warrior Programs. Kathy brings a powerful testimony of unconditional love and forgiveness that shines through the darkness as a ray of hope. She has a strong connection with women and wives struggling with the pain and heartache in the wake of PTSD. She speaks publicly as a wife and a mother who fought the war with the symptoms in her husband and came out the other side with a restored relationship with Chad and an even stronger faith. It was Kathy's love and faith all along that kept the Robichaux family together, and subsequently the Mighty Oaks Foundation was born. Kathy has a unique knowledge of PTSD. She speaks to women with a powerful message of God's grace, forgiveness, and moving forward. She has reached the hearts of many women through her faith, public speaking, and the Mighty Oaks Warriors Programs by effectively healing lives for the glory of God.

Chad & Kathy Dating in 1994

Kathy as a High School Cheerleader

1st USMC Birthday Ball as "boyfriend / girlfriend" - 1994

Chad at USMC Boot Camp 1993

Traditional Marine Corps Wedding in Sun City, Ca. - 1995

USMC Birthday Ball at 3rd Force Recon Company - 1999

Chad & Kathy Skydiving in 2001

Chad with Special Operations Teammate, Eastern Afghanistan - 2004

Chad vs Andrew Yates, World Series of Fighting, NBC Sports - 2013
**Photo Credit: Lucas Noonan, WSOF*

Chad vs Humberto Deleon, StrikeForce at Houston Toyota Center - 2010
*(Mentioned in Week 1) *Photo Credit: Sherdog.com*

(bottom left)
Another MMA Victory.
Chad giving glory to God!
**Photo Credit: Lucas Noonan, WSOF*

(top left)
Haili and Daddy - 2015

(top right)
Hunter and Mommy - 2015

(middle left)
Father's Day picture to Chad while away in Afghanistan - 2006

(below)
The "Robo" Family
Chad, Kathy, Hunter, Haili and Hayden
2015

The "Robo" Boys in Brazilian Jiu-Jitsu Gis

Chad and Mighty Oaks Alumni at the USMC Wounded Warrior Battalion Birthday Ball 2014

Chad & Kathy Teaching in 2015

Chad & Kathy in 2014

20th Anniversary Marriage Vow Renewal with Jeremy & Susanne Stalnecker in the Bahamas - 2015

ACKNOWLEDGMENTS

We are so grateful to the many people that God has brought alongside us to encourage us and believe in us through our journey from the ashes...as we stepped out on the water and believed in firm ground under our feet.

Neither of us could be here today, nor would we have ever seen this book come to life, had it not been for each of your obedient following to God's call to join us in the fight for His people in this broken world in which we all live.

It is our prayer that God will use *Marriage Advance*, and His story through our life, as a tool to restore lives, families and legacies... and have an eternal impact on The Kingdom of Heaven. We thank you for being part of making that possible.

We still pray for our marriage daily and hope to continue to see others rise from the ashes and become mighty oaks of righteousness, *a blessing for The Lord's splendor.*

We love you all,
Chad & Kathy Robichaux

References

[1] Stormie Omartian, *The Power of a Praying* (Harvest House Publishers, 1996)

[2] Dave Ramsey, *Financial Peace University* (The Lampo Group 1749 Mallory Lane, Brentwood , TN 37027)

[3] *Guys and Dolls* (music and lyrics by Frank Loesser and book by Jo Swerling and Abe Burrows, 1950)

[4] Teen Sex: John S. Santelli, *The Association of Sexual Behaviors with Socioeconomic Status, family Structure and Race/Ethnicity among US Adolescents* (American Journal of Public Health 90, 2000)

Robert L Fllewelling and Karl E. Bauman, *Family Structure as a Predictor of Initial Substance Use and Sexual Intercourse in Early Adolescence* (Journal of Marriage and Family 52,1990)

[5] Drop out of High School: Sara McLanahan, Sara and Gary Sandefur, *Growing up with a Single Parent: What Hurts, What Helps* (Cambridge: Harvard University Press 1994)

[6] Pregnancy: Kristen A. Moore et al., *A Statistical Portrait of Adolescent Sex, Contraception, and Childbearing* (National Campaign to Prevent Teen Pregnancy, March 1998)

[7] Crime: Glenn T. Stanton, *Why Marriage Matters: What's Marriage Got to Do With It?*

[8] Drugs and alcohol: *National Longitudinal Survey of Adolescent Health* (Wave I, 1995)

Judith Wallerstein, Julia M. Lewis and Sandra Blakeslee, *The Unexpected Legacy of Divorce: A 25 Year Landmark Study* (New York : Hyperion, September 2000)

General reference for page 104: *United Families International* http://unitedfamilies.org/

[9] Sanctus Real, *Lead Me* (Writer(s): Matt Hammitt, Jason Ingram, Chris Rohman, Windsor Hill Music, Sony/ATV Timber Publishing, West Main Music)

[10] Research by Louann Brizendine at the University of California.

[11] Gary Chapman, *The Five Love Languages: How to Express Heartfelt Commitment to Your Mate* (Northfield Publishing, 1995)

General reference: *Veteran Suicide Information*
Suicide Data Report, Department of Defense (DoD) 2014 Suicide Report (http://www.suicideoutreach.org/Docs/suicide-data/DoD-Quarterly-Suicide-Report-CY2014-Q1.pdf)

Suicide Data Report, 2012 Department of Veterans Affairs, Mental Health Services, Suicide Prevention Program, Janet Kemp, RN PhD, Robert Bossarte, PhD (http://www.va.gov/opa/docs/suicidedata-report-2012-final.pdf)

General reference: *Veteran Divorce Information*
A Marine's Guide To Marriage Success, The Official Website of The United States Marine Corps (http://www.mcaspendleton.marines.mil/Chaplain/MarriageGuide.aspx)

SPEAKING ENGAGEMENTS

To book Chad and Kathy to speak at your church, special event, or to lead a marriage program, seminar, or weekend, visit:

www.MightyOaksPrograms.org/Speakers

Testimonials of just some of the pastors who have utilized Chad and Kathy to minister to their congregations:

"Chad and Kathy first visited The Life Church in May of 2014. We were expecting an engaging presentation to honor veterans for Memorial Day, but we received so much more. There was so much depth to their presentation about life's challenges and how to overcome those challenges with Jesus Christ as our ultimate Healer. Chad and Kathy's personal testimony showed our congregation how to have victory over so many of life's entanglements, from depression to marital struggles, and how Jesus can be our bondage breaker. We now consider this amazing couple part of The Life Church Family!"
– David Baird, Pastor, The Life Church (Manassas, VA)

"With disarming honesty and faith, Chad and Kathy Robichaux have shared their story here in Brentwood. And God has used their story to rekindle faith and hope in weary hearts, and rekindle love in tired marriages."
– Dave Mason, Pastor, Brentwood Neighborhood Church (Brentwood, CA)

"I have yet to see anyone in public speaking have such a dynamic effect on people that causes them to make such radical but positive changes in their lives. Chad Robichaux's integrity, his trustworthiness and faithfulness to all that he does, has been a fantastic influence on our leadership team and on the church as a whole."
– Ron Woods, Lead Pastor, The Assembly (Broken Arrow, OK)

Chad and Kathy Robichaux are the founders of Mighty Oaks Warrior Programs. The mission of Mighty Oaks is to operate on a standing commitment to reach the brokenhearted, with a specific calling to assist our nation's military Warriors and families find a new life purpose through a hope in Christ, after enduring hardship through their service to America.

OUR PROGRAMS

FIGHT CLUB FOR MEN: THE QUEST FOR AUTHENTIC MANHOOD

Our six-day intensive peer to peer program serves as the catalyst to help warriors discover the answers to the big questions in life. Challenges related to the struggles of daily military life, combat deployments and the symptoms of post-traumatic stress (PTS) surface during these six days, and Fight Club for Men teaches how to fight through these challenges.

FIGHT CLUB FOR WOMEN: FINDING THE VIRTUOUS WOMAN

Fight Club for Women is a process of learning to become a Virtuous Woman – the "Proverbs 31" woman. This five-day retreat leads spouses and Military women through a time of learning, exploration and growth.

MARRIAGE ADVANCE: LOVE NEVER GIVES UP

Our four day Marriage Advance Program is designed for couples to gain a better understanding of the struggles they each face. We structure conversations around needs, expectations, goals and forgiveness to help couples move forward.

To support or learn more please visit:

www.MightyOaksPrograms.org

An official program of Serving California

THE MIGHTY OAKS JOURNEY

Mighty Oaks Warrior Programs (MOWP) is committed to serving the brokenhearted by providing intensive peer-based discipleship through a series of programs, outpost meetings, and speaking events. Our Fight Club and Marriage Advance Programs take place at SkyRose Ranch in Central California and run from four to seven days to ensure that each participant is focused solely on his or her recovery and identifying purpose moving forward. All warriors and spouses are fully sponsored for the programs, travel, meals, and lodging expenses.

MOWP began as a grassroots ministry out of WoodsEdge Community Church in Texas and is a story of God's transformational power to turn tragedy to triumph. It is a journey starting with one man's brokenness after war, one woman's willingness to fight for her family, their faith in God's promise that we can rise from the ashes and be Mighty Oaks of Righteousness…and the obedience of all those who have followed that have been bold enough to pursue God's call.

Chad and Kathy's testimony of overcoming the challenges posed by post-traumatic stress disorder (PTSD) after Chad's service in the War on Terror led to their calling to assist individuals who are going through the same struggles. In the moment Chad felt called to this work, he realized he wasn't alone in his suffering. Countless other combat veterans faced the same challenges he did, ending in 23 suicides a day and a divorce rate of over 80%. Chad wondered, "Why doesn't someone do something about this?" Eventually, he realized that the answer was clear…"Why not me?"

Many great men stepped up to mentor Chad and Kathy through their struggles, but none have been more prominent than Steve Toth and Pastor Jeff Wells of WoodsEdge Community Church. It was through this church that Chad and Kathy were later ordained and commissioned as ministers by Pastor Jeff and sent to begin the Mighty Oaks ministry to America's military warriors and families. Mighty Oaks continues to preserve their foundational values with a grassroots approach, while operating on a national level to empower veterans to begin healing and have a positive impact on the world around them.

In 2011, the stage was set for the first Men's Fight Club to take place in Westcliffe, Colorado, with all non-active duty veterans. The initial Mighty Oaks' Fight Clubs served alongside Dave Roever's Foundation and would later become Mighty Oaks Warrior Programs. As new warriors attended Mighty Oaks Programs, they continued to find hope and purpose beyond their service. Being challenged by a peer-to-peer model while they grab hold of a future worth living again, the warriors continued to rise to the challenge. As the warriors completed each Fight Club, they sent their brothers…this organic process evoked rapid growth! That growth led to a shift from the veteran community to an open door to reach active duty service members. We soon began to receive Marines, Sailors, and Soldiers on official "military orders." In 2012, during this time of explosive growth and with increasing demand from the U.S. Marine Corps Wounded Warrior Battalion West, Dave Roever introduced Chad to B. Wayne Hughes, Jr. Together, they explored the possibility of taking Mighty Oaks to El Paso De Robles, California, which translates to "the path of the oaks." (We say this was a wink from God himself!) Wayne wanted to see The Lord's hand over our returning American warriors, and he hoped to develop a veteran's program at his ranch. Wayne loved the program and agreed to build a lodge to host Mighty Oaks. The timing of this blessing could not have been better. A partnership between Mighty Oaks and Serving California was formed, and SkyRose Lodge was built. Thus, SkyRose became the host home of the Mighty Oaks Warrior Programs and the growing influx of warriors and military families.

Today, Mighty Oaks has completely merged to become Serving California's Mighty Oaks Warrior Programs and calls California home; however, we are now empowering the alumni to establish pre and post-care "outposts" across the country as well as a networked mentorship program.

The Mighty Oaks Warrior Programs began with one church, as the local ministry of a family who wanted to help others in the same way that they had been helped in their fight against the challenges of this world. We have expanded our locations, but our vision remains the same: to serve others by challenging, equipping, and empowering them to, in turn, reach others suffering in the same way. Since 2011, we have served hundreds of warriors and have not lost one alumnus to suicide. We continue to work toward eradicating the horrific, national veteran suicide rate of 23 per day. Together, we can all strive toward the common goal of ending the war at home by finding hope and a future by aligning with the very purpose for which God created us. We will continue to lead others to rise from the ashes and become Mighty Oaks!

Fully paid scholarships are available through Serving California for all MOWP programs for active duty or veteran military personnel, as well as their spouses, by applying online.
For more information on programs or on how you can participate in donating or supporting MOWP, visit…

www.MightyOaksPrograms.org

Notes

NOTES

NOTES

Notes

Notes

Notes

Notes

Notes

Notes

Notes